Advance Praise for *The Dangers of Pimento Cheese*

"There are other stroke survivor memoirs out there, but none funnier. Andy was a writer before he had a stroke, not because he had one. And though the story he brings back is at times sorrowful, his great writing— alternately wise-ass, droll, emotional—keeps you from ever feeling sorry for him."

—Luke Sullivan, author of *30 Rooms to Hide In: Insanity, Addiction, and Rock 'n' Roll in the Shadow of the Mayo Clinic*

"Ten years ago, Andy Ellis suffered a stroke that took away his mobility on the left side of his body, but it didn't take away his humor and the gratitude he greets the world with every morning. *The Dangers of Pimento Cheese* is a memoir, a stroke survivor's guidebook and a cookbook for living a 'new normal' life after a devastating challenge. Read it and be transformed."

—Alice Osborn, author of *Heroes without Capes*

"*Warning!* Laughing out loud may occur while reading this memoir. Recovery post-stroke is no laughing matter. The author cleverly demonstrates the power of humor to neutralize anger and despair and to expedite the ongoing process of healthy adaptation."

—Cynthia L. Frazier, PhD, clinical psychologist

"We all have a journey full of chance and choice. Many people unconsciously choose to play the victim and plague themselves with excuses. Then there are those who consciously choose to be vulnerable, choose to be courageous, and choose to persevere. Andy's journey is just that. Whether you've had a debilitating condition or not, you will find this an inspiring read full of raw perspective and seasoned in humor. Thank you for this gift Andy, you are 'one of the white hats.'"

—Ronnie Neal, wellness coach and personal trainer

"Andy Ellis' *Pimento Cheese* offers a poignant and honest glimpse into the patient side of medicine. His candidness and sense of humor helps ease the frustration, loss of dignity and dependence associated with a devastating stroke. His story will be truly inspiring to family, caregivers, and especially patients as they see that a successful recovery is not necessarily a return to normal but a return to a 'new normal' way of interacting with the world."

—Susan A Glenn, MD, PhD, Raleigh Neurology

"They say until you experience something you can't quite comprehend the magnitude of pain and suffering, as well as joy someone can go through. Andy shares all and gives hope to anyone who has gone through a serious illness with setbacks. He knows gratitude and strength. I thoroughly enjoyed getting a better glimpse into his life and feel privileged to call him a friend."

—Suzanne B. Lucey, bookseller, Page 158 Books

The
DANGERS
of
PIMENTO
CHEESE

The

DANGERS

of

PIMENTO

CHEESE

*Surviving a Stroke South of
the Mason-Dixon Line*

Andy Ellis

THE DANGERS OF PIMENTO CHEESE
SURVIVING A STROKE SOUTH OF THE MASON-DIXON LINE

iUniverse books may be ordered through booksellers or by contacting:

iUniverse
1663 Liberty Drive
Bloomington, IN 47403
www.iuniverse.com
1-800-Authors (1-800-288-4677)

ISBN: 978-1-5320-0148-2 (sc)
ISBN: 978-1-5320-0149-9 (e)

Library of Congress Control Number: 2016912048

Print information available on the last page.

iUniverse rev. date: 08/22/2016

For Cristie, of course

I must be willing to give up what I am in
order to become what I will be.
—Albert Einstein

Contents

Introduction

Okay, I'll admit I'm nowhere close to being the most Internet-savvy person on Earth. But over the last ten years I've used Google, Yahoo, Bing, Ask, Lycos, ChaCha, DuckDuckGo, and every other search engine out there trying to find a link between ingesting a pimento cheese sandwich (on King's Hawaiian Bread) and having a full-blown stroke just minutes later. And I can find zero evidence. So should I type "The End" and call the book quits here?

And what if the International Dairy Foods Association gets wind of the fact that I am besmirching what I once read a *Southern Living* editor refer to as "hillbilly pâté"? I was raised on the stuff. Both of my grandmothers, as well as my own mother, made pimento cheese at home, hand-grating the cheese, draining the pimentos, and using the hand mixer, usually reserved for cake mixes, to create this delicious spread. The last thing I want is the Pimento Cheese Defamation League on my ass because I suggested hillbilly pâté is the reason I now walk with a cane and get really good parking spaces anywhere I go.

But what if I have it totally backward? What if the stroke train had already left the station and was heading to my brain before I ate that sandwich and pimento cheese is the sole reason I'm still on earth today? What if pimento cheese somehow has the same chemical components as heparin, the clot-buster drug I received immediately upon arriving in the emergency room and is what actually saved my life? Trust me—I've Googled, Yahooed, Blinged, Asked, Lycosed, ChaChaed and DuckDuckGone these questions as well. Again, I can find no evidence.

The good news is I'm not lactose intolerant, nor do I suffer from turophobia, the legitimate fear of cheese. Yes, I have eaten pimento cheese many, many times since having my stroke—I live life on the edge. In fact, I had a delicious pimento cheese and avocado omelet just two weeks ago. I highly recommend this combination, especially with sausage and a biscuit (truly southern).

But I didn't set out to write this book to discuss what I like to eat. Rather I was encouraged to share my story as a stroke victim, patient and survivor by numerous doctors, therapists, nurses and other medical professionals. Each of whom encouraged me to write something with the hope of helping or encouraging other patients and the families and caregivers of those who have suffered a stroke.

Some might find my light, sometimes humorous tone to be disrespectful to those who have suffered a totally debilitating stroke or, worse, have died from one. That is certainly not my intent. Come on, I threw dice on the sidewalk outside death's door myself.

The number one thing you need to know and understand is this was *not* written by a doctor or someone with any medical education whatsoever. I am *a* person who had *a* stroke. And from what I understand, no two strokes are alike. Hence, my symptoms belong to me. While in the hospital, I met several other men who'd had strokes, and some of us did share causes and some symptoms. But there were different levels of severity and after effects.

So *please* do not take this account of my stroke as the medical definition of what a stroke is. I highly suggest you visit the American Stroke Association website at strokeassociation.org or the National Stroke Association site at stroke.org to learn symptoms, causes and ways to prevent a stroke.

The intent of this book is not to say, *Hey, here's what I went through. Oh, poor me.* Rather my aim is to say that a stroke, like other disabling medical events from a heart attack to an amputation, is life changing, and here's how I have dealt and continue to deal with it. My psychologist once said to me, "The psychological corollary to physical healing is adapting."

That's probably the primary message I'm trying to convey. Several things in my day-to-day life have been affected as a result of my stroke. I can't change things back to the way they were pre-stroke and, to some degree, I don't want to. I am healthier now than I was then and am probably a better person. I am more appreciative, quicker to count my blessings, and rarely take anyone or anything for granted. I'm certainly not a saint, but I am enjoying life more, even when my disability occasionally tries to trip me up. And more importantly, I'm a person who has relearned how to be, more or less, independent.

I've divided this book into three basic chunks. First are my tips for managing hospital life immediately following a stroke. Next are my observations about returning to day-to-day life after being released from the hospital. And finally, I share where I stand nearly ten years after eating that dastardly sandwich.

CHUNK #1

I DIDN'T EVEN HEAR THE SIREN

I May Have Had Chips with That Sandwich—Frankly, I Just Don't Recall

It was the thirty-fifth day of the new year, an unusually warm day even for the rather mild winter of 2005/06. A winter when children comfortably rode their new two-wheelers outside on Christmas afternoon. I was living on a farm in Ashland, Virginia, in a small cottage I referred to as the Mouse House (a.k.a. TMH) because the entire dwelling was about seven hundred square feet, perfect for a good-size, rent-paying mouse. Oddly enough, the lease I signed for TMH specified that I was responsible for the feeding and care of the farm's barn cat. And for the entire two years I lived there, I never saw evidence of a single mouse except for the grisly remains of one little fella the cat had gifted me and left on the front porch.

My wife, Cristie, was traveling back and forth between Ashland and her historic family home she had inherited just outside Raleigh, North Carolina. I was wrapping up some business projects in Richmond and had plans to move down to North Carolina in early spring. Our marriage meant being together only on weekends; either she'd come up to Ashland or I'd drive to Wake Forest, the town where the college was founded before it was moved to Winston-Salem in the 1950s. This particular weekend, Cristie did the commuting, and for many, many reasons that will soon become clear, thank God I wasn't the one on the road that Saturday.

It was early afternoon, and I had made a pimento cheese sandwich for each of us. We were sitting in the living room of TMH. Upon finishing the sandwich, I lit a cigarette, like I did following nearly every meal. While I

3

was puffing away, Cristie asked me a question about what DVD we wanted to watch that night.

Thanks to Netflix, we had three disks to choose from; this was prior to streaming Netflix. And as I gave my opinion on or voted for my choice of film, Cristie said, "I can't understand you." Thinking that perhaps I was still chewing my last bite of sandwich, I pardoned myself for talking with my mouth full and repeated my statement. Again, she couldn't understand me. Now I was thinking maybe she didn't care for my movie choice and was just messing with me. But then the mood of the conversation darkened dramatically.

Looking a bit alarmed, Cristie said, "Something's wrong with your face."

I thought, *This is my face. If she doesn't like it, she should have thought about that before she married me.*

"Your eye and your mouth over there (pointing to the left side of my face) are droopy. And your speech is all slurred. I think you're having a stroke." She then got up, walked over to me, took the cigarette (the last one I did or will ever have) out of my hand, and snubbed it out in the ashtray. A ton of thoughts quickly raced through my head. Allow me to list them for you.

- *A stroke? When did my beloved wife become an MD?* To my knowledge, no one in her family had had a stroke. Nor did I recall our ever watching a DVD or one of those made-for-TV movies on *Lifetime* where Meredith Baxter's character's husband (probably played by Mandy Patinkin) has a stroke while they are going through a divorce. And would watching said movie give my wife her knowledge of stroke symptoms?
- *A stroke? Come on. I am feeling no pain at all.* At the time, I didn't know the signs of a stroke, but isn't a stroke supposed to hurt? If not, why do they always lump it together with heart attack? You know, "Taking this pill greatly reduces you risk of heart attack and stroke. Be sure to ask your doctor if this pill is right for you." We've all heard these lines dozens of times. And we've all seen enough episodes of *ER* and *Grey's Anatomy* to know a heart attack

4

must be rather painful (victims grabbing their chests with their eyes bugging out of their heads). Hence, a stroke must, at least, be up there with, at the very least, getting a splinter. Me, that day? No pain. Suddenly, I felt a little sleepy. But it was a Saturday afternoon and everyone knows God created Saturday afternoons specifically for taking naps and shopping at Best Buy for large appliances. I spoke with a well-educated theologian who assures me God did not create Saturday afternoons for yardwork, despite what Home Depot and Lowe's ads tell you.

Let me interject here that perhaps if I'd seen my drooping face and had the blinding headache that many stroke victims experience, I would have believed my wife's prognosis. But instead, when she said she was going to call 911, I stupidly said (and I'm dead serious here), "If you love me, you won't call 911." Dumbest words to ever leave this droopy mouth.

I digress.

- *A stroke? For Pete's sake, I'm forty-nine years old and in fairly good health.* Okay, as you already know, I smoked. And in addition, I drank, and I was a bit overweight, but not fat. My cholesterol was … I didn't know; I'd never had it checked (little did I know, but it was well over 200). Blood pressure, low (more about that later). No diabetes. While I work in advertising, a profession known for tight deadlines and high stress, I was and am self-employed and can monitor just how much stress I'm willing to deal with. The greatest stress I had experienced that past year was being a Baltimore Ravens fan.

These would be the last coherent thoughts I'd have for the next several days. I may be totally wrong. In truth, I probably wasn't conscious for a good four days or so. I asked my wife what she did during that time, and she said, "I just kept asking your neurologist if you (meaning *me*) were going to be okay … over and over and over again." I was later told by my speech pathologist that, upon arriving at the hospital, I received a flu shot. It seems that during the previous winter, this hospital had had a serious outbreak of the flu and was taking extra precautions in 2006.

So, like I stated, I wasn't on this planet for several days. From what I'm told, those days were filled with a battery of tests and a lot of time in the world of radiology (CAT scans, MRIs, and so on). I have zero recollection of this. And if you've ever had an MRI, your first one is pretty hard to forget (it's like listening to Skrillex with a jackhammer accompaniment at an eardrum-bursting volume). When I did touch down back on earth, the first thing I recall is being extremely thirsty, yet everyone seemed worried about my ability to swallow. I recall at one point going to radiology and having to drink some vile-tasting liquid as they performed some kind of scan of me swallowing this crap. Thus I was given unnaturally thickened liquids. There was this powdered goop that was added to apple juice, cranberry juice, or water to make it easier for me to swallow and lessen my chances of choking. It didn't taste all that great, but at least I had something cold and wet in my mouth. It took virtually no time to get used to it.

Food was another story. I'm still not certain if it was the stroke or not smoking or exactly why everything tasted differently to me. Eating (manipulating food in my mouth) was a bit challenging. Identifying what I was eating was even more challenging, and I'm not making some clichéd "hospital food" joke here, I swear.

It was very early on when I met my speech pathologist and therapist. She was a wonderful, kind, perfumed woman whom Cristie had met upon arriving in the emergency room. Weeks later, during a speech therapy session, she told me that once they wheeled me out of the ER, Cristie broke down and they hugged.

Once I started to get my bearings and somewhat understood what was up and down, I was in a single-bed room on the second floor of Henrico Doctors' Hospital in Richmond, Virginia. This was basically a step-down room, similar to where patients go after being graduated from the ICU. I had an oxygen tube in my nose, a respiration monitor taped to a finger, a few wires attached to my chest, a catheter with a Foley bag for urinating, and a couple of IV lines going into my arm, eventually replaced with a PICC line just below my right collarbone. I recall being in constant fear of tangling things up or pulling something off or, even worse, out. What hadn't even come close to registering in my semi-feeble, drug-numbed brain was the severity of the situation. I thought they were just going to watch me for a day or two and then send me merrily back home to the farm, where I'd go back to writing commercials and newspaper ads.

"Easy tiger," said my lovely bride, "you're going to be here awhile."

Everything I Knew about the Hospital I Learned from My Son

I feel somehow obligated to provide a bit of pre-stroke hospital experience. In 1985, my then wife gave birth to our son, Graham. It was an uneventful birth that took place on the same day as the Live Aid concerts event organized by Sir Bob Geldof and Midge Ure to raise funds for Ethiopian famine relief. Graham entered this world as the Pretenders were performing "Back on the Chain Gang."

When he was a little over five months old, Graham's day-care director took his mom and me aside to tell us she thought there was something wrong with Graham in terms of how he was developing. He was behind other children his age, and the director suggested we talk with our pediatrician. Graham's doctor had been my pediatrician when I was a child and was a family friend of my parents. He was unsure what or even if there was an issue but suggested that we see a pediatric neurologist at the Medical College of Virginia.

When I walked into the doctor's office, the first thing that struck me was the fact that he was David Letterman's doppelganger. But he turned out not to be nearly as funny. It took him virtually no time to examine our son and diagnose him with a developmental delay, which is just a more palatable way of saying cerebral palsy.

I recall my throat going as dry as a Southern Baptist wedding and all the color draining out of my wife's face. I knew immediately I had more questions than our one-hour appointment would afford. I didn't know where to start and feared I'd ask the least important questions first. The most important questions would have been about quality of life, life expectancy, treatments and therapies. One of the last questions to come into my head was my ex's first. "What caused this?" From what I understand, this is a very common and appropriate maternal response.

This was also the day I got really, really pissed with God. How could a loving, caring God allow such a thing to happen to an innocent, beautiful child? God and I had another come-to-Jesus moment three years later when Graham started having severe seizures and was diagnosed with epilepsy.

This was when the hospital visits first started. Graham spent a week in Children's Hospital of Richmond with EEG electrodes glued all over his head while a medical technician flashed a strobe light in his face to induce seizures in a controlled environment. His mom and I took turns staying overnight with our son, a scenario that would be replayed dozens upon dozens of times over the next several years.

Graham has been hospitalized several times for seizure observation. He's had scoliosis surgery, both hips replaced, kidney stones removed and far too many other procedures to mention. The truth is, I can't recall them all, but I'd be willing to bet his mother can.

At the time of my stroke, Graham was living with his mom on the southside of Richmond. Cristie phoned her to let her know what had happened and explained that the next child support check would be a tad late. My ex graciously said not to worry about child support anymore because Graham would be turning twenty-one in five months and child support would be replaced by disability. I do regret Graham never came to see me in the hospital. Perhaps his mom thought it might scare or confuse him. Or maybe she rightfully thought that the last thing Graham needed was to spend one more second in a hospital when he didn't need to be there. Or maybe it's just because I never thought to invite him to visit, assuming he and his mom had far more important things to do.

The point is thanks to Graham, I had some knowledge of how hospitals operate (get it?) prior to being admitted into the hospital following my stroke. I'd learned a lot of the terminology and acronyms. I learned that not a lot happens on weekends and if you need something or someone, expect to wait. And I learned that the expression "You catch more flies with honey than you do with vinegar" applies more to hospital personnel than to Department of Motor Vehicles employees or telemarketers.

But perhaps the most important lesson I learned was that no matter how tough of a day I was having in the hospital, my son had been through far worse. And he usually did so with a smile on his face.

Keep Your Friends Close and
Your Medical Personnel Closer

Many, many years ago (pre-stroke) on a flight from Richmond to San Diego for a job interview, I read Mark McCormack's *What They Don't Teach You at Harvard Business School,* a remarkably informative and useful best-seller. It was kind of a contemporary version of Dale Carnegie's *How to Win Friends and Influence People.* One lesson gained from *Harvard Business School* that I've never forgotten is to make people working for you or on your behalf feel incredibly important. Play up to their egos and grant them superpowers.

I put this lesson into practice immediately upon arriving at a hotel in Southern California. I needed to change clothes prior to my interview, yet my room wouldn't be ready for an hour or two. I went back to the guest service rep at the front desk (I still recall the name on his badge—Bob), and I said, "Bob, I have a problem, and you're the only person on earth who can help me." I wasn't lying. Only Bob could bump me into the next available, cleaned room. I explained about the job interview and needing to clean up after a long flight. Poof! Ten minutes later, I was in a nice room with a king-sized bed overlooking an inlet filled with sailboats. Ten minutes after that, I was in a cab on my way to an interview for a job that I eventually turned down because I wasn't ready to move to the West Coast.

There's something you should know about me: I dislike being waited on by anyone, from bellmen to waitresses to valet parking attendants. But in the hospital, I was in a physical and mental condition where I had no choice but to allow others to do things for me. If this was going to be my lot, I was going to be damn sure that those taking care of me knew they were appreciated. It's not like I could leave them a 20 percent tip versus a 15 percent one. If the hospital had paid me a nickel for every time I said "thank you" while I was a patient there, there would have been no reason for them to have submitted an invoice to Anthem Blue Cross/Blue Shield. It would have been a wash. But it's vital to me that every single person who received a "thank you" from me knew it was sincere and heartfelt.

I made it my mission to make these individuals feel important, special and appreciated. And, in addition, I wanted the time they had to spend with me to be somewhat enjoyable. So I tried to be entertaining or, at the very least, somewhat funny.

For example, I had two male nurses, Nathan and Adam, who'd tend to my meds and vitals and stuff at night, but they never worked the same shift on the same nights. However, they did know each other and were friends. So what I'd do is give them both an equally hard (but joking) time. Nathan would give me a shot in my hip and I'd say, "Jeez, that hurt, Nathan! It never hurts when Adam does it." Or I'd say, "Adam, Nathan crushes up my pills into much smaller pieces and mixes them in with vanilla pudding. You always put the pills in applesauce. Are you hoarding my pudding, man?" This would always get a laugh, and I always had fun figuring out ways to tease them. It was also a good exercise for my damaged brain.

My humor wasn't reserved for male nurses. I tried for weeks to convince the female nurses who bathed me in the evenings to stop using the phrase "private parts" and replace it with the British expression "naughty bits." My success rate was less than 30 percent, but they giggled all the same.

This brings up a point about hospitals and extended medical care in general. Anyone who is admitted should be prepared to lose all sense of modesty. You reach a point where it just doesn't matter anymore what anybody sees. I recall one day when there appeared to be some blood in my Foley bag, and there was a discussion about whether or not my catheter needed changing. This discussion didn't get settled during normal business hours. Around ten o'clock that night, I found myself lying on my back in my bed with my hospital gown pulled up to my chest while six female nurses stood around the bed debating whether it should come out or not. Who was going to do the deed of removal, and who would get the honor of inserting a new one? As with a lot of memories I have of this time, my memory of this event may be exaggerated. I hope this actually happened as I recall and it wasn't some sort of really, really sick erotic dream I had. I was on a lot of meds.

In a similar vein, I recall one day shortly after starting rehab when my physical therapist was trying to teach me how to transfer from my wheelchair to the bed. She was holding my gait belt (basically a durable, thick, two-inch-wide, cloth belt with a metal buckle that goes around a patient's waist and gives the care provider something substantial to hold onto during a transfer) as I stood and basically collapsed onto the bed. This was not what my PT was aiming for. We had practiced this several times, and I just wasn't transferring well. On this particular attempt, a nurse was standing in my room waiting to give me my meds and heard this brief little exchange between my therapist and me:

PT (in a Shakespearian aside): What's it going to take for me to get Mr. Ellis into bed?

Me: I suggest taking me out for drinks first.

Nurse: (*Laughter and blushing*)

This brings up one of the biggest struggles I had the entire time I was in the hospital, which was getting the staff to stop calling me Mr. Ellis. I mean, come on, after the last two tales I shared, you'd think the ladies and I would be on a first-name basis or perhaps have nicknames for each other. At first, a few staffers reluctantly started calling me Andrew, but it took weeks before Andy was the universally accepted moniker for the boy.

One gentleman quickly understood I wanted to be one of the guys and not some special hospital patient. Carlos was in charge of radiology transportation. This strapping Latino from the Bronx quickly became my buddy, my pal, my friend after escorting me on numerous (nearly daily, at first) trips to the land of CT scans, MRIs and regular old x-rays. If the situation had been different, I could have imagined him as my personal trainer. But in this instance, Carlos was like my personal mental trainer. He was my good dose of testosterone—a man's man who'd give me the soul handshake with a solid grip, never treating me like I had any sort of weakness, all the while aware I wasn't well. Even on days when he wasn't tasked with wheeling me somewhere, he'd show up in the doorway of my room just to say hi. Above all, Carlos was my cheerleader, frequently checking on my progress at the nurses' station and encouraging me to work even harder. He was there for me from day two to the day I left.

One day, I called Carlos "one of the white hats." He replied, "What the hell does that mean?" I asked, "Did you ever watch cowboy TV shows or movies when you were a kid?" He explained that wasn't part of his culture growing up in New York. So I explained that in old cowboy movies, the bad guys always wore black hats while the good guys wore white ones and that if he had been a cowboy, he'd be one of the white hats. He seemed to like that and smiled every time I called him by his adopted name. I recall him giving me a hug and fearing he'd crush me.

The only thing that bothered me about Carlos was that he reeked of cigarettes. Now, it had been a couple of weeks since my last smoke, and while I probably hadn't 100 percent kicked the habit, the smell of cigarettes was growing more and more unpleasant to me every day.

This brings up a point that's bothered me for many months since the stroke. Between the times I was wheeled outside to get fresh air on warm days and times I've entered various hospitals as an outpatient rehab person, I've seen people—seemingly intelligent, grown adults—standing outside in all sorts of weather donning their open-back hospital gowns. They've been connected via plastic tubes in one arm to liquid-filled bags hanging from portable IV trees with the other arm, bending at the elbow to raise a Marlboro to their lips.

My mother, who smoked until the day she died, used an expression in talking about ex-smokers who'd try to convince her to quit, saying, "No one hath more virtue than a reformed whore." Quite frankly, I could give a rat's ass if they smoked. I've never said one word to any of these puffers, but it took me no time to realize my pack-a-day habit wasn't going to get me back on my feet. Plus, I quickly garnered that smoking had contributed to landing me in that Hill-Rom bed. So, with deep regrets to the stockholders of Richmond's own Philip Morris, I proclaimed myself a quitter.

I promise to discuss more about the hospital staff, but per this chapter's title, I need to also discuss friends and family.

When my ex-wife and I divorced, we both sort of learned who our true friends were. Some people sided with one of the two of us, and then some friends, appropriately, remained friends with each of us individually. I can't speak for my ex-wife, but it certainly opened my eyes.

Having a stroke definitively opened my eyes as to just *how many* friends I have. And I was astounded. My father used to say, "If you can count your friends on one hand, you're doing pretty damn well." Dad, you should be very proud of your son.

Cards and flowers began arriving immediately, many from people I hadn't heard from or spoken to in quite some time. At first, Cristie rightfully asked people not to come to the hospital. The doctors and nurses were keeping me pretty busy, and the time I did spend in my room was spent sleeping or watching TV.

In fact, it probably wasn't until week three, once I moved to the fourth floor, that visitors were allowed to come by my room. This caused quite a bit of confusion for some folks. Henrico Doctors' Hospital has two campuses in Richmond, one on Parham Road and a second on Forest Avenue. The Forest campus is known by more people because it has the Women's Pavilion, which practically every woman in Richmond over age thirty has visited at least once, plus it's pretty well known for its cardiology department and staff. Hence, while I was lying in room 408 on Parham Road, many of my friends were making a new friend in room 408 on Forest. And this was despite how specific Cristie was with people on the phone.

Cristie would spend nearly all day with me at the hospital fielding phone calls, calling the nurse when my IV feeder machine would beep (which for a couple of days was nearly every five minutes), filling out my menu for the next day, working on that day's Sudoku in the newspaper and changing the water in the vases. Initially she slept in a chair and then a rollaway bed next to my hospital bed until I got my bearings, but she eventually started retiring to the Mouse House after I had dinner. The problem was she'd head home to have a glass of wine and relax, but there would be twenty-two phone messages waiting for her. So she'd spend the evening reporting to relatives and friends about how I was doing. I think she needed rest even more than I did. But she was great, and I grew deeper and deeper in love with her. Mind you, my speech was still pretty messed up, and I'd try to say things like, "Ife truve yug." I meant every word.

Perhaps everyone experiences this after going through a serious, life-threatening situation, but I went from a non-touchy-feely, semi-emotional person to an outright "I love you, dear friend. Give me a hug," sort of guy with every friend who came to visit. And there were many.

There was Bill in his black leather jacket who'd come in, sit in the chair at the foot of my bed, and just talk with me. I had had a chance to become friends with Bill over a decade prior and didn't do so. I lost a great deal of time that I could have spent conversing, sharing and learning from this gentleman who is smart, funny and remarkably caring. Bill is a public relations guy who can talk to absolutely anyone. He's also a great cook who has a personal chef business (I was promptly corrected when I referred to it as catering) with a friend. When he learned that my nurse's son was going to culinary school, the two of them formed a bond, with Bill reassuring my nurse that her son could work on a cruise ship or at a resort or a restaurant, which made her feel great about her son's future. Plus Bill would also come visit prepared with the latest news and gossip from the Richmond advertising world.

And then there was my long-time, truly goofy friend, Craig. Craig is the most naturally funny person I've ever met. This is not to say Craig can tell a joke, because he can't, but he tells tales about his family, his work, and himself that are self-deprecating and hilariously funny. Many stories are quite scatological; others downright crude.

I recall returning to my room late one afternoon after a session of occupational therapy, and on the wall to the left of my bed was a poster of about a dozen scantily-clad young women. Written in lipstick on the poster was, "Hurry up and get well. We miss you—the girls from the office." I noticed in the bottom left-hand corner in small type, it said, "The Girls of Vivid." It wasn't until I got out of the hospital and returned to my office that I was able to Google "The Girls of Vivid," and learned that Vivid is a porn video firm. But Craig had bought the poster, borrowed his wife's lipstick, and posted the nearly R-rated masterpiece in my room in my absence. Male nurses would come in and say stuff like, "Jesus, I wish I worked at *your* office," while female nurses or therapists would say things like, "Yeah, I bet you *do* want to get back to work."

Craig visited frequently and was always able to make me laugh. He would also eat any food I might have left on my tray.

Most Sunday evenings, my musician-business friend Carlos (not to be confused with radiology transportation Carlos) would stop by, and we'd watch *Extreme Makeover: Home Edition,* which was pretty schmaltzy but better than *The Amazing Race,* and I could rarely stay awake long enough to finish *Sunday Night Football.* We always had good conversations, and he'd also fill me in on what was going on with mutual friends and contemporary culture. I remember his visits fondly and look forward to getting together with him to this day.

My sister drove up from Cary, North Carolina, to see me, meaning she put in a good five-plus hours on the highway to visit with me for three hours. This touched me deeply. Thinking I needed all the luck I could get, she gifted me with a four-leaf clover in Lucite. In retrospect, my sister's visits (she came a second time, as well) were bittersweet as she would pass away nine months later of a heart attack.

A couple of friends from our days in Baltimore were kind enough to drive down to visit. I think these folks came more to give Cristie support and encouragement, which I truly appreciated.

And then there were some people who came by who were obviously uncomfortable to be there. For some, just being inside a hospital is creepy. It could bring back memories of visiting a loved one who passed away or a time they were sick in a hospital as children. Some friends who didn't come to see me in the hospital have since said they were worried I might not have recognized them (stroke = brain injury) and I'd be embarrassed. In truth, the opposite happened.

Other people have told me they feared they might be interrupting therapy, sleep or a meal if they came by. It was easy to tell those who were anxious to leave as soon as they got there, and I can understand it. I've felt the same way visiting friends in hospitals since the stroke, and while I feel I should be some "hospital pro" offering my friends insightful encouragement, I'm anxious to get out of there. I even had one friend come to visit me on a Saturday evening smelling of wine and acting tipsy. The point is just because people don't come to visit you in the hospital or only stay for five minutes constantly checking their watches, it doesn't mean they don't care.

Friends bearing gifts were also interesting. As I mentioned, my sister brought me a four-leaf clover in Lucite, and my friend Craig brought me a poster of porn starlets. Craig also brought me a Bernese Mountain puppy plush toy that he named Lucky. So between the shamrock and a stuffed animal, two people who were dear to me thought what I needed to get better was luck. I think I'm *lucky* they weren't my doctors.

This reminds me of the visitors who came to see me every Thursday afternoon. I think it was my second week on the rehab floor when I was wheeled back to my room a little earlier than normal. And it was around four o'clock when this woman came into my room with a golden retriever. My wife and I had had to say good-bye to our dog the previous autumn, so having a therapy dog come pay a visit brightened my day tremendously. Over the remaining weeks at Henrico Doctors', a dog would come by for a thirty-minute visit every Thursday. Most were on the smaller side (not from the AKC Toy Group) and were able to climb onto my bed. I recall a couple of them falling asleep at my side. But being a big dog (large breed) person, my favorites were the golden who first came to visit and a black lab, who I believe was my final therapy pup.

Anyway, back to my two-legged visitors. Knowing I'm an avid reader, several people brought me books. And while it was thoughtful and appreciated, it presented two problems. One, I was still a bit fuzzy-headed, so comprehension and retention were a bit on the low side; and two, with my entire left side paralyzed, holding a book with my left hand was next to impossible. It's still difficult, and when I do read an actual book, I set it on a table, hold it open with my left arm, and turn the pages with my right hand—which is why I normally read books today using a tablet. I've become so accustomed to reading on an e-reader that when I do read an actual *book* book, I frequently look at the top of the printed page to see what time it is and feel both disappointed and foolish when I do.

Some friends brought me food. The best was the peach-strawberry-banana smoothies my former coworker Chuck would bring me from Tropical Smoothie Café. A friend from Baltimore brought chicken curry from Café Zen and conned a nurse into microwaving it. I seem to have a penchant for cafés.

Other people loaned me DVDs, MP3 players, and other stuff we spent a good month after leaving the hospital returning to their rightful owners.

But the best thing anybody could bring me was news of what was going on in life outside the hospital. I needed to know I would be able to relate to my post-stroke world, that not everything had changed. Just me.

Just Say "Huh?" to Drugs

It was probably about three to four weeks after taking up residence at Henrico Doctors' Hospital that I was cognitive enough to ask what all the pills were that I was ingesting multiple times a day. Dose one came when I was at breakfast. Dose two was midway through morning therapy, and dose three was near dinner. And finally, I got dose four sometime after I'd fallen asleep for the night (i.e., "Mr. Ellis, wake up. Wake up, Mr. Ellis. Time for your meds."). To avoid choking, they'd grind up my pills and stir them in with pudding or applesauce.

When I finally became curious as to what role each capsule or tablet played in my daily well-being—or eventual survival—I discovered that there was a blood thinner, a sleep aid, assorted supplements and Prilosec to help my stomach deal with the pharmaceutical Whitman's Sampler I was ingesting four times a day. But what confused me was the fact they also had me on *two* antidepressants twice a day.

Once I finally had the wherewithal to pose the question, I asked, "Hey, what's with the antidepressants?" It was explained to me that people who survive a stroke tend to sink into a state of depression. My immediate thought was, *What happens to those who* don't *survive a stroke? What kind of antidepressants do they serve in the hereafter? They must get the* really *good stuff.*

Here it is now, ten years since the stroke, and I still take ten different meds a day. And a couple of the prescriptions I'm on today are a result of how long I was in the hospital. Physicians of nearly every discipline, short of OB/GYN, ran a battery of tests on me, and a few of them found additional issues. For instance, it turns out my heart doesn't pump what's deemed as

20

the appropriate volume of blood to all parts of my body (also known as heart failure); hence I was put on carvedilol (brand name Coreg) and had a heart catheterization. I also was diagnosed with avascular necrosis, and an orthopaedic surgeon put me on the osteoporosis medication Fosamax. This was an experimental drug therapy based on a study conducted in Japan, and my ortho doc wanted me to try it. This totally confused my pharmacist, who only saw women in their sixties come into CVS with a script for Fosamax.

Let's get back to the antidepressants. I dislike them because they make me feel emotionally numb. I've always been a fairly emotional being. I can be easily moved by a song, movie, book or YouTube video, and this has been amplified since the stroke. Many stroke survivors have to deal with a condition called pseudobulbar affect, or PBA. The symptoms are unpredictable crying, laughing, or other emotional episodes that come out of the blue and can be inappropriate at times (kind of like Tourette syndrome without the swearing). I seriously doubt I suffer from PBA; maybe I'm just more emotional than most. But I can deal with weepiness far more easily than feeling flat on antidepressants.

But I'd be lying if I said I don't get down sometimes, and I do so more frequently than prior to the stroke. Depression? I'm not sure I'd use that word because the people I've known with clinical depression are frequently debilitated. I don't get so down that I can't get out of bed or work. I think that, rather than suffering from depression, I suffer from frustration. But I don't think GlaxoSmithKline has a pill for that yet. The frustration stems from the cruel little jokes the stroke played on my body. And those jokes can change from day to day.

The first time my sister came to visit me in the hospital, she gave Cristie a silver bracelet engraved with the Alcoholics Anonymous motto, "One Day at a Time." Given the stress and worry my beloved bride was going through at the time, the bracelet was a very appropriate and appreciated gift.

However, I need to make a point that for a stroke *survivor*, life isn't "One Day at a Time." It's more like, "One Day as It Presents Itself." There are days when things are firing on all cylinders but others when I'm backfiring, sputtering and choking down a potted, gravel road. The truth of the matter is there are some days when my speech is less discernable than others, when my limp is more pronounced than others, and my left arm is too hypertonic (an exaggerated degree of muscular tension) to be of much use. And for the life of me, I can't tell you why one day serves up a big helping of aggravation and the next day doesn't.

I admit that on more than one of those days, I've actually uttered the words, "I am sick of being me." And that's from a person who could and should spend every waking hour counting his blessings. I'm not on disability; I'm not living in an assisted-living facility; I can bathe, dress, feed and drive myself. But I can also get frustrated.

I recall one day a few weeks after I'd started occupational therapy and was trying to pick up coins off a table with my left hand. I said in a moment of frustration, "This is a total pain in the ass." I thought I'd said it so under my breath no one could have possibly heard me. Following lunch, when I'd normally go back into the rehab gym for afternoon therapies, I was wheeled back to my room where I was soon joined by a young woman who introduced herself as the resident psychologist. She said she was called because I'd had an outburst during my morning therapy. I sighed and asked, "An outburst?" She took off her glasses and, while nervously tapping one earpiece on the side of her Diet Coke can, she said, "I'm told you swore in the rehab gym this morning?" I had to think really hard to remember having said anything, and finally recalled having said, "This is a total pain in the ass." I told her this hardly seemed like anything resembling an outburst. In reality, if I'd been honest, I would have told her I'd wanted to *scream* at the top of my lungs, "Why can't I get my fucking left hand to work?!" We talked a bit longer. She repeatedly stated that she wanted me to go back on antidepressants, but I fought her and she relinquished. I saw her here and there on my floor during the rest of my stay, and she always had a Diet Coke and would ask, "How are you doing, Mr. Andrews?"—something I'm sure a lot of people with the first name Andrew get as well.

Here I am several years down the road and, while I still get frequent bouts of frustration, I am no longer on antidepressants. Instead, I see a psychologist once a week (this one drinks hot tea rather than Diet Coke and, while she wears glasses, she doesn't tap her earpiece against her mug), and I've done so for the past several years. I can only imagine how tired she must be of my lugging in the same suitcase of frustrations over and over again. In a sense, this is kind of the opposite of an antidepressant because, rather than masking or numbing my emotions, I'm actually more in touch with them, which allows me to admit my frustrations and grants me permission to get good and pissed off from time to time.

I do wonder about possible repercussions of taking so many drugs for such a long period of time. I guess I just have to trust my doctors and the people at CVS to make sure I'm not walking some pharmaceutical tightrope.

God Bless You, Philo Farnsworth

There's an old joke that goes, if television is so bad for you, why do they have one in every hospital room?

If one is to believe Wikipedia, it was Utah's own Philo Farnsworth who invented not only the first complete all-electronic television system but also the video camera tube. So if TV is indeed bad for you, you can shake your fist at Mr. Farnsworth.

In truth, in 2012, the University of Queensland studied some twelve thousand Australian adults and concluded that "every hour of television watched after age 25 reduces the viewer's life expectancy by nearly 22 minutes." Well, thank goodness I wasn't in a hospital Down Under—because watching TV seriously helped me through the countless nights I spent in my hospital bed.

And it just happened to be a great couple of months of television. The day after my stroke, the Pittsburgh Steelers defeated the Seattle Seahawks twenty-one to ten in Super Bowl XL (meaning 40, not extra-large). Mind you, that game and I were on two different planets on February 5, 2006.

However, five days later, I believe I joined Katie, Matt, Bob, and other NBC notables as they covered the Winter Olympics in Turin, Italy. That was sixteen days of skating, skiing, sledding and Canadians putting the rock in the house (curling). It transported me out of Henrico Doctors'.

Speaking of competitions, that winter saw the premiere of season two of *Dancing with the Stars*, a show that boggled my brain even prior to the stroke

THE DANGERS OF PIMENTO CHEESE

as I found it difficult to identify many of the so-called stars. That season, the only two personalities I'd even heard of were George Hamilton and Tatum O'Neal. And they weren't exactly A-listers. My nurse's aide Jewel loved the show. She was the poor soul who was given the task of giving me my evening sponge baths, and she'd schedule my bath for whatever time it was that *DWTS* (as those in the know call it) came on because, despite the fact I didn't care for the show, I'd turn it on for her. Jewel is one of the sweetest people I've ever met in my life, and she'd finish my baths by covering me in baby powder. In fact, there were some nights when I looked like something off the blooper reel from *Scarface*. But I don't think I'll ever smell baby powder again and not think of Jewel.

And speaking of movies, on the first Sunday in March we celebrated the 78th Annual Academy Awards with a small party in my room. As is custom, we had our "who can predict the winner in the most categories" competition where everyone puts five dollars in the pot and the winner gets the cash prize. My friend Carlos (not to be confused with my radiology buddy, Carlos), who frequently stopped by on Sunday evenings for a visit, was coerced into playing this game and left several hours later less a five-spot. My sister joined us from North Carolina via phone. Cristie had gone to Joe's Market (now known as Libbie Market) and snuck in some gourmet treats. It was a great, fun night for me and probably an even better night for the folks behind *Brokeback Mountain* and *Crash*.

However, I did make a horrible television mistake one Sunday evening in early March. Not sleepy quite yet, I started flipping through the channels around ten o'clock and stumbled upon something called *Grey's Anatomy* on ABC. Upon my first five minutes of viewing, I thought, *Hey, this takes place in a hospital. I'm in a hospital; I should be able to relate to this.* With no disrespect to absolutely anyone who's tended to my care, health, well-being, and recovery (in my heart, you are the most beautiful people on earth), my interns and residents weren't quite as pretty as Ellen Pompeo, Katherine Heigl, or, for that matter, Patrick Dempsey. Plus, as these surgeons-in-training worked their way to becoming actual surgeons, a lot of their patients were finding their way to the basement with tags around their big toes. While I was never under the care of a sawbones, I imagined how many trips the elevator just outside my room had made to Henrico Doctors' morgue. This tweaked the show from a medical drama to a medical horror with lots of bodily fluids and bacteria being swapped among the pretty docs in supply closets.

It wasn't until three weeks prior to being released that I discovered the secret of surviving in a hospital room for months. Ladies and gentlemen, I give you *The Travel Channel*! I first discovered it on a Sunday afternoon. They were airing something on the best beach getaways in North America, and I mentally escaped to each one of them. *The Travel Channel* was my introduction to something I never thought I'd ever be interested in—cruising. I have always had a love of the ocean and the beach and have vacationed in the Outer Banks of North Carolina at least once a year every year of my life since I was two. The whole notion of being on a floating resort hotel never found its way onto my radar until *The Travel Channel* aired something like five back-to-back shows on different cruise lines one weekend afternoon. From Cunard's elegant *Queen Mary 2* to the family-friendly Disney Cruise Line (where I have a vision of playing blackjack in a smoky casino with a liquored-up Chip 'n' Dale), I suddenly found the appeal of sailing the open sea. I have since sailed with Holland America Line (HAL) to the western Caribbean, Alaska and taken a magnificent cruise from Quebec City to Fort Lauderdale in autumn, when the leaves were changing in Canada and New England. I think the appeal for me is that it's like staying in a very nice luxury hotel that changes locations overnight, every night. And just so you know, I have found cruising to be very handicap-friendly, at least on HAL.

So here's my advice for you: should you have a stroke and find yourself conscious inside an ambulance, ask one of the EMTs these two questions: (1) "What hospital are we going to?" and (2) "Do they have *The Travel Channel* (or at the very least *Destination America Channel*)? If not, please find a hospital that does and go there." Or I guess you could wear a medical alert bracelet with information to that effect.

Despite What My Ex-Wife Might Tell You, Yes, I Do Have a Heart

I'm not sure if it was for insurance reasons or what, but the longer I stayed in the hospital, the more tests they ran on me and the more things they found wrong. For example, following a fall in the bathroom off the therapy gym, I was x-rayed from head to toe. When they reached my left hip, they noticed that the bone density wasn't what it should be. I was diagnosed with avascular necrosis, which is caused by a lack of blood supply to an area of bone tissue. This meant a hip replacement was inevitable.

Another morning, a young lab coat (my nickname for any medical tech person) came into my room with a large machine on wheels and started taping electrodes to my chest to administer an EKG. The guy barely said two words to me. Then that afternoon, a small Asian doctor stopped me while I was shuffling back to my room with my occupational therapist and a walker. His tidings of good cheer were once I was released from Henrico Doctors' Parham facility, I would be going to Henrico Doctors' Forest campus for a heart catheterization. The issue was that my heart was not pumping out as much blood as it should, and he wanted to see if there was some sort of blockage. If so, it might require putting a stent in my heart. This news devastated me. I broke down crying. My occupational therapist and Cristie were in my room with me, and my therapist, seeing how upset I was, asked if she could pray for me. She led us in a prayer, which made me cry even harder.

The fact was I was seeing a light at the end of my hospital tunnel. I could walk with a walker and things were progressing with all of my therapies. So just when I thought I might be hugging my nurses and therapists good-bye, I learned there was a whole new issue to address. Plus the thought of taking a video camera through my groin (femoral artery—thank you, WebMD) and into my heart gave me the willies. "And Mr. Ellis, you'll be awake the whole time so you can watch your heart on the video monitor." *And why should this make me happy, small Asian doctor?*

As my discharge from Parham Road grew closer, my anxiety about the heart procedure grew as well. It was a bright near-spring Friday afternoon when I was set free and told to report to the Forest campus. Both Cristie and I had expected an ambulance or some other mode of medical transportation to ferry me from Henrico Doctors' A to Henrico Doctors' B, but no. Cristie had to drive me herself in her 2003 electric-blue Mini Cooper. Halfway there, she and I shared sort of a *Thelma and Louise* moment of, "To hell with this, let's make a run for the border." But, fearing small Asian doctor might have been onto something, clearer heads prevailed, and off to Forest Avenue we went.

Upon reporting to my room (complete with a roommate and an unpleasant odor), my vitals were taken and the nurse administering my vitals freaked out because my blood pressure was for some unknown reason alarmingly low. Mind you, I felt fine, however less so when the nurse said, "I don't want to alarm you, but this is life threatening." To prove it, they brought in the defibrillator, followed by several other very serious-looking lab coats. The good news was I was immediately moved to a private room. They basically positioned the bed so that my feet were much higher than my head, and I was eventually proclaimed "absent of the forest" (or out of the woods). No one ever explained to me what had happened and, once stabilized, no one seemed concerned.

I slept pretty well that night until I woke up remembering that my heart was going to make its television debut in a few short hours. Given how my low blood pressure had sent everyone into a lather the day before, I feared that the anxiousness I was feeling now would send my blood pressure through the ceiling and then we'd all enjoy a screening of *The Return of the Defibrillator* (imagine those last five words in sort of a dripping blood kind of horror-movie font).

So eight in the morning came, and I was wheeled into the Cath Lab on a gurney and given some mild sedative. It's important you know that I cannot verify my memory of my time spent in said Cath Lab with 100 percent accuracy. But I do recall three things rather vividly: (1) The room was far less high-tech than I imagined it would be. I was expecting something more futuristic with more beeping, flashing diodes and whirring servos. (2) While I don't recall them actually feeding the catheter into my femoral artery, I clearly remember looking at my own heart pumping from the inside and being both freaked out and astounded. I kind of wanted to ask the tech administering the procedure, "Is that really *my* heart, or do you guys have some looping video feed of one guy's heart and you just play the same video for everybody?" However, I was told to be as still and quiet as possible, so I kept my conspiracy theory to myself. Perhaps Oliver Stone will one day uncover this charade and prove me right. Anyway, while watching my heart do the cardio-rumba, no one in the lab was doing anything like pointing at the monitor and screaming, "What in God's name is that!" In fact, the people in the lab didn't appear to be doing much of anything except for— (3) The big guy with a Styrofoam take-out container loaded with scrambled eggs, greasy link sausages, hash browns and Texas toast was talking with his mouth full. And while his big country breakfast smelled delicious, it looked like the sort of meal, if eaten regularly, would lead you *here*. This image continues to haunt me to this day as I wonder just how appropriate it is to eat while performing a medical procedure—even on a Saturday. The good news is there was no blockage and no further procedures were necessary.

I was put on the prescription drug carvedilol, commonly used to treat high blood pressure and heart failure; told to see a cardiologist annually; and, ladies and gentlemen, I was discharged from the hospital that afternoon!

Heading Home

It's odd to me that I have relatively zero memory of returning to the Mouse House. Why don't I remember such a momentous occasion? However, I do recall a few weeks prior in the hospital discussing whether living in TMH and eventually moving to Wake Forest would be plausible. I was still in the wheelchair and needed help with nearly every day-to-day activity. Would it make more sense to go to an assisted-living facility and continue rehabilitation there until I became more mobile?

There were several variables to take into consideration. The Mouse House as well as the house in Wake Forest are both one floor only (two steps to get in the back door in Wake Forest). Good. Wheelchair accessible. Was outpatient therapy available and convenient? Yes. In fact, the rehab facility in Virginia was only a few steps from a Curves fitness center that Cristie belonged to, so she could exercise while I rehabbed. Could Cristie physically care for me? Yes. I still relied on a wheelchair, but transferring from the chair to the bed, toilet, car, and bath chair, while requiring assistance, was going much better and safer. It was decided I could head home.

Before I left Henrico Doctors' Parham, the Diet Coke-loving psychologist paid me a final visit to discuss marriage, patience and, yet again, a prescription for an antidepressant. Right off the bat, I told her I wouldn't fill any prescription she wrote for me. But I listened intently as she warned me that returning to what I probably perceived as life as usual wasn't going to be anything close to what it had been. Her sternest warning was how hard an event like this is on a marriage.

While I was in the hospital, a friend of mine living in Florida asked a friend of his in Richmond who was a stroke survivor to visit me. He and his wife came to the hospital one Saturday afternoon. And even though we'd never met before, we've remained in touch. It was about six months after getting out of the hospital I learned this couple was divorcing. I mentioned this to one of my physical therapists (now in North Carolina), saying it made me sad, to which she explained divorce is very common among post-stroke couples.

This worried me. My love for my wife had intensified since the stroke. I mean, come on—the only reason you're reading these words is the fact that she called 911. But by the same token, I'm no longer the same man she originally married. So what if Cristie had thoughts like *This isn't what I signed on for* or *Where is the guy I married seventeen years ago?*

Being the curious journalism major I am, I started investigating, and found some alarming statistics. In the 1970s, the post-brain incident divorce rate was at 40 percent, actually below the national average for divorces in general. But by the 1980s, that divorce rate had increased and ranged from 48 to 78 percent.

If you think about it, those numbers shouldn't be all that startling. The spouse has to take over several responsibilities the stroke survivor used to manage. Many stroke survivors are unable to return to work, which can lead to financial stress. And daily fears and frustrations can make the survivor irritable and not much fun to be around.

Being a caregiver is a tough, selfless job. As I've mentioned before, I dislike having people wait on me. So when I got home and had to rely on my wife to help me with basically everything, I felt bad. If she so much as sighed once, I'd put off asking for the next thing I needed for as long as possible.

I finally moved to Wake Forest in late summer of 2006. I know Cristie was glad to be home, and she was soon able to return to her job as a grant writer. We hired a student from the seminary to drive me to my therapy appointments, and, little by little, I was getting stronger. My physical therapist at the time was a petite, eight-month-pregnant woman, and I was scared to death, as we were becoming less and less dependent on walkers and quad canes in therapy, I was going to fall on her. I believe it was just before Halloween when she gave me my first traditional cane. As I wrote that last sentence, tears came to my eyes. I guess that's probably one of the most significant benchmarks in my stroke recovery.

With very little help from occupational therapy in this regard, it was the following month when I returned to the kitchen. Early on in my recovery, I was asked what hobbies I have, and I stated cooking was probably my main hobby. So I found it odd that there was only one day in an outpatient therapy session where the therapist and I spent the morning in a mock kitchen. I know Cristie was as glad as I was when I was able to cook again. Let it be known, she's not a bad cook. If I have one criticism of her cooking skills, it's that she's too ambitious. When she cooks, she frequently chooses recipes that sound great but have far too many steps and require too many bowls, pans, pots, measuring cups and other assorted tools. Sometimes it takes just as much time to clean up as it does to prepare the dish—which is usually delicious, but way too much work. I can see why she doesn't enjoy cooking. I, however, do enjoy it. I select far simpler recipes and clean as I go. I'm a big fan of the slow cooker. A three-pound boneless turkey breast, half a cup of chicken broth, a few herbs, and seven hours in a slow cooker, and you've got an entrée that's good for at least two meals and maybe two turkey sandwiches. I also have a triad of tasty grilled salmon (rich in omega-3, vitamin D and selenium) recipes I rotate. And come autumn and winter, chili and corn bread are frequently on the menu. So I'm hoping as long as I keep feeding her, Cristie won't file for divorce.

Mind you, everything hasn't been smooth sailing. We've hit some snags along the way, and I'm willing to blame myself for most of them. It's usually on frustration days when I declare that I'm sick of being me. I'm a bit more sensitive than I was pre-stroke and can easily get my feelings hurt. Those moments are when "unable" teeters into the realm of "incapable". Then I get defensive, and that doesn't get us anywhere.

In spring of 2015, Cristie had surgery on her right foot to correct a toe she'd broken years ago that didn't heal properly. It was getting more and more uncomfortable for her when wearing shoes. Following surgery, she needed a few days in bed with her foot elevated and iced. I was delighted for the opportunity to put the caregiver shoe on the other foot, figuratively speaking. I took her to the outpatient surgery facility and lovingly reassured her everything would go fine and that I'd try to take care of her as well she's taken care of me. I say that because there are plenty of areas where I still need her help. My favorite moment in Cristie's Franken-foot adventure was just prior to wheeling her into the operating room after she'd been lightly sedated and was starting to grow impatient about waiting so long. With sedation clouding the "grammar and tense" part of her brain, my lovely bride proclaimed, "I want to be do."

Prior to her surgery, I sat down and seriously asked myself what was the one thing I could do to best help Cristie. The answer I came up with was to answer every request she might have with the word *sure*. And while there were a few times when I was physically unable to keep my promise, I think I gave Cristie fairly good care. And I've since tried to make *sure* a habit.

I mentioned that occupational therapy didn't really cover returning to the kitchen. Another topic that was equally dismissed was intimacy. I mentioned this to my psychologist, and she was shocked, stating this was a gross oversight. Perhaps this was something the Henrico Doctors' psychologist was supposed to take up with me but chose not to because she was ticked off because I'd refused her antidepressants. "This will fix Mr. Andrews. I'll ruin his sex life. That'll give him something to be depressed about."

All relationships take work. Throw in a monkey wrench like a stroke, and the work required multiplies dramatically. But we've gotten better and better at shooting a flare into the sky when either one of us is getting stressed, frustrated, or generally pissed. It's all about defusing any problems before they become outright issues.

CHUNK #2

UNABLE AND INCAPABLE AREN'T SYNONYMS

Try This at Home

I figured somewhere in this missive I should include a recipe for pimento cheese if for no other reason than so my non-Southern friends can taste the joy that is this Dixie staple. This recipe is a combination of my mother's recipe (which I'm sure was her mother's) and *Southern Living* magazine's. I can't be responsible if someone has a stroke after eating pimento cheese, but I swear it's highly unlikely. And while it's great on King's Hawaiian Bread, it's also good on Triscuits or Ak-Mak crackers and great in an omelet with avocado.

 Southern-Style Pimento Cheese

Ingredients:

2 cups shredded extra sharp New York* cheddar cheese

8 ounces cream cheese, softened

1/2 cup mayonnaise (my grandmother made her own from scratch, but Hellmann's or Duke's will work—*not* Miracle Whip)

pinch of garlic powder

1/4 teaspoon onion powder

1/4 teaspoon ground cayenne (optional, but it adds a nice little kick)

1 (4-ounce) jar diced pimentos, drained

sea salt and fresh ground black pepper to taste

(*how ironic)

Instructions:

In a large bowl, mix the cheddar cheese, cream cheese, mayonnaise, garlic and onion powder, cayenne, and pimentos using a stand or hand mixer, beating at medium speed until thoroughly combined. Season to taste with salt and pepper.

Frustrations and Fears

I assume most stroke survivors experience an aha moment or, as I refer to it, the *okay, now I get how it's going to be from here on out* realization. I can't recall exactly when it happened to me. But I do recall wanting to do something I'd done a million times before, and my brain said *Yeah, sure, we know how to do that,* but my body told my brain, *You know, you aren't nearly as smart as you think you are.*

What frustrations and fears I have are directly related to my physical limitations. Since my stroke was in the right hemisphere of my brain, I have physical deficits on the left side of my body. Fortunately, I've always been right handed.

Prior to the stroke, I had an injury to my right ankle. It was the evening of Friday the thirteenth in June 2003. While running to my car in the rain, I slipped, fell, and twisted my right ankle so severely my foot, which should have been sticking up at twelve o'clock, was grotesquely set at five. Hence I had emergency surgery that night and woke up with a number of screws and pins in my ankle. Actually, I was wheeled into the operating room at 11:50 p.m. and specifically asked the surgeon to wait until midnight to start because I was now officially superstitious regarding Friday the thirteenth. While he was already pissed off with me because he had a tee time at seven thirty the next morning and this bit of surgery was going to take a few hours, he agreed to wait until it was officially Saturday the fourteenth and sacrifice his golf game.

Despite extensive outpatient physical therapy following the surgery, exactly how much my screw-and-pin-enriched ankle would slow me down wasn't officially demonstrated until a couple of months later. I was crossing a street in downtown Richmond, Virginia, as the "walk/don't walk" light started blinking "don't walk" and I attempted to run, only to discover that running was no longer an option for my right ankle. So even prior to the stroke, I wasn't 100 percent mobile.

When someone recently asked why I periodically get frustrated, I explained that some tasks in the pre-stroke world were a straight line from A to B, but in the post-stroke world, that line looks like it was drawn by a deranged chimp with an Etch-O-Sketch. In other words, some things take more time, effort and energy. The act of getting in and out of a shower takes every ounce of concentration I can muster to avoid falling.

I once asked my neurologist why I feel so drained at the end of the day, and she explained I now have to seriously focus on things that were once quite routine and accomplished by rote. Applying that much mental energy to even mundane tasks taxes the brain.

Post-stroke, I definitively have a limp on my left side and what I call partial paralysis in my left arm and hand. In a manner of speaking, my left hand is my Achilles heel. It basically has two grip strengths: (1) barely holding on at all and (2) cybernetic killer kung-fu grip.

I heard an interview on NPR in spring 2013 with a man who'd had cancer in his arm that was spreading rapidly. So the doctors amputated his arm just above the elbow. At the time of the interview, the man was working with doctors at Johns Hopkins and trying out a robotic arm that operated via sensors in his brain. As he explained it, if he wanted to move his fingers to hold something, all he had to do was think about it. Initially, he said he had to really concentrate, but as time went on, things became more fluid and natural.

In a sense, I could relate to this gentleman because picking up something with my left hand requires intense concentration; it doesn't come naturally to me anymore. And for some reason, letting go requires even more focus.

An additional issue is the fact that I can't turn my left wrist very well. For instance, I am unable to turn my wrist so my palm is turned up to the sky. Alas, it's a good thing I can still make a living as a writer because I'd suck at panhandling.

So for the most part, my frustrations have to do with my left hand. What I need to acknowledge is that people who have lost mobility in their right arms and hands have a totally different set of issues. And for those who have lost mobility on their dominant side, I can't imagine the difficulties or amount of therapy required to totally change the way one functions.

Here, in no particular order, are things that vex me.

- *Saran Wrap* or any plastic wrap for that matter. Even pre-stroke, I found this product tricky to deal with, frequently ending up with a wadded ball of clear plastic. Now with limited strength in my left hand, dealing with the stuff is even more challenging. And I hate besmirching the product because it's been getting a lot of crap lately about plastic wrap being unsafe for use in a microwave, when in truth the FDA deems the product okay but suggests venting (puncturing) the wrap prior to zapping. However, it isn't wise to microwave plastic storage bags, plastic bags from grocery stores, takeout containers, water bottles or plastic tubs (i.e., containers for whipped topping, margarine, cream cheese, etc.). And the folks at SC Johnson (A Family Company) can thank me later.

- *Plastic bottles* are being made using less and less plastic these days. Why? Because it weighs less, costs less to make and ship, and earns significantly greater profits for beverage companies. They're doing the exact same thing with their aluminum can cousins. My problem/frustration is that to open that plastic water/juice/tea bottle, I have to hold it with my left hand and twist off the cap with my right. To effectively hold the bottle stationary, I have to use the cybernetic killer kung-fu grip I mentioned earlier. And as the plastic gets thinner and thinner, the more water/juice/tea ends up on the table or on my pants. What I've learned to do is to hold the bottle just below the neck and, rather than squeezing the bottle, I push down to hold it still on a counter while I twist off the cap. Aluminum cans don't trouble me nearly as much since I can pop open a can using just my right hand.

- *Doorknobs* when I'm holding something in my right hand. I can't effectively grasp and turn a doorknob with my left hand. Hence, I have to set down whatever I'm holding or transfer it to my left hand and turn the knob with my right hand. But that only works if I'm holding something unbreakable because if I'm holding, say, a glass or a coffee mug containing some liquid, there is a decent chance I'll drop it. The same goes for plates or anything breakable. This frustrates not only me but my poor dog as well because everyone knows a door is what a dog always wants to be on the opposite side of. So my dog, who'll be nosing a door in hopes it's not shut tight, has to wait for me to set down whatever it is I'm holding and then come back and open the door.

- *Flossing* is a task requiring two hands. Fortunately, someone has created these little things called flossers or floss picks that can be effectively used with one hand. I had a conversation with my current dentist in which she asked me if oral health was discussed while I was in the hospital. And my answer was, "Other than encouraging me to brush my teeth twice a day, no." She was truly discouraged and proceeded to give me a lesson on the relationship between oral health and overall wellness. The Mayo Clinic website confirms her claims that poor oral hygiene can lead to heart/cardiovascular disease, pregnancy and birth weight problems, osteoporosis and other health issues. So the drawer next to my sink is home to a bag containing dozens of those green flossers.

- *Cutting onions, tomatoes, and other round fruits and vegetables.* As I stated, I enjoy cooking, and during the nine months of 2006 that I was unable to function in a kitchen, I sorely missed it. I also think my ability and willingness to both cook and do the grocery shopping are two reasons Cristie hasn't given me the boot. I have a set of very good, professional knives, but as good and as sharp as they are, they don't prevent round edibles from rolling away. Yes, I have seen some adaptive cutting boards where you basically impale the spherical foodstuff on a skewer protruding up from the board. Or you could DIY and just buy a wooden cutting board at Target then swing by Home Depot or Lowe's for a large nail. For some reason, either way, I feel the integrity of the food has been compromised and I still can't cut the entire edible orb. So I either ask Cristie to dice and slice or use a mandoline or food processor.

- *Bruised hands* are a fairly common part of my appearance. This is because I use my arms to a tremendous degree to help with my balance. As a result, my arms are rarely at my side. I'm not implying that I look like I'm attempting to fly or am doing an impersonation of the late Joe Cocker, but I frequently hit the top of my hands (the left one more frequently than the right) while passing a table, counter or doorknob. Since it doesn't really hurt all that much, I frequently forget I bashed my hand and am surprised to discover a rather substantial bruise there a day or two later. I'm certain being on a blood thinner enhances the black and blueness of these bruises. Maybe I should invent bubble wrap gloves.

- *Drive-through windows, ATMs, toll booths and letter boxes* are unusable for me. I've had bank tellers ask why I physically come inside their branch to make a deposit rather than use the ATM or drive-through (please note I didn't spell it *thru*, for the same reason I don't drink *lite* beer). The last thing I want to do is make the teller uncomfortable by explaining that I have partial paralysis in my left arm and using these conveniences is inconvenient for me. The good news here is that I don't do fast-food restaurants, so a drive-through Big Mac isn't an issue. Then there's the issue at the post office. Outside my local post office are two large, blue letter boxes where people can pull up to and deposit letters or small, flat packages. Or if you're me, you pull up to the box, put your car in park, open the car door, bang the side mirror on the driver's side door against the letter box, swear, get out of the car and deposit the letter right-handed. Alternative number two is to park in the post office parking lot, go inside, and slip the letter in the outgoing mail slot.

My biggest frustration, however, is toll booths. The quickest way to get from downtown Richmond, Virginia, to southside

Richmond involves a number of toll booths. I know this because I frequently work in Richmond, and the partner I work with lives in Midlothian, just south of Richmond. I can't roll down my window, hand the attendant cash, or throw coins into the basket with my left hand, roll up the window, and proceed on my way. I used to have an EZ Pass transponder, but I wasn't using it enough to satisfy the people at the Virginia Department of Transportation and they canceled my account.

I'll tell you, a GPS device is a must-have for drivers with only one functioning hand, not only because you can't steer and hold a map or printed directions but because you can program the GPS to find a route that doesn't include toll roads. But be warned, the first time I took a non-toll road route from downtown to southside, Ellen (my nickname for my Magellan GPS) took me through some rather dicey neighborhoods. Next time I'll see where my smartphone leads me.

What I've neglected to share here is that upon finishing in-patient rehab at Henrico Doctors', I was given two parting gifts. One was basically a round yellow sponge on the end of a white plastic stick so I could wash my back. The other is called a Duro-Med 32 Aluminum Reach with Magnetic Tip. Basically, it's a thirty-two-inch-long stick with a gripper on one end and a handle with a trigger on the other end that opens and closes the gripper. And at the end by the gripper, there's a tiny magnet that can pick up a small screw or safety pin (i.e., something small, very lightweight and metallic; in truth it rarely works). I guess I could use this at the bank or post office, but they've been so kind as to supply me with convenient handicapped parking spaces, it'd be rude not to use them.

- *Sloppy speech*, or what I sometimes call stroke mouth, is another frustration. The first therapist I met with following the stroke was a speech pathologist. Her job was to test my ability to speak clearly, as well as look for any cognitive issues. I really enjoyed the cognitive tests because they were basically riddles, trivia games, and interpreting sentences that might have more than one meaning. For example, the difference between "She was a light housekeeper" and "She was a lighthouse keeper" could be confused when spoken. On the other hand, my speech wasn't horrible, but I did initially have to work at enunciating slowly and deliberately. And to this day, if I'm tired or feel stressed, the timbre of my speech goes higher and enunciation gets sloppy. This frustrates me frequently when I'm on the phone with someone who doesn't know me, and the person I'm speaking to keeps repeating "Sorry," "Pardon?" or "What?" I think a good part of my frustration is that I can feel the other person's frustration trying to understand Mr. Sloppy Mouth.

This brings us to other fears, starting with the biggie.

- *Fear of falling.* Because of where the stroke was in my brain, I have proprioception issues. According to Nobel laureate Sir Charles Scott Sherrington's 1906 publication *The Integrative Action of the Nervous System,* "the initiation of proprioception is the activation of a proprioreceptor in the periphery. The proprioceptive sense is believed to be composed of information from sensory neurons located in the inner ear (motion and orientation) and in the stretch receptors located in the muscles and the joint-supporting ligaments (stance)." In other words, it's the brain and body's ability to understand where one is in space or in any particular environment. And to not get too medical on you, I suck at it. Proprioception is what the police officer is checking when he or she conducts a field sobriety test (e.g., close your eyes and touch your finger to your nose). Closing my eyes or walking into a dark room throws me off completely. This is why I have a bath chair in the shower and request one when I stay in hotels. When I close my eyes while shampooing what little hair I have left, I'm basically looking to fall.
  In November 2007, a good year and nine months following the stroke, I was going to bed one Saturday night, walked into the dark bedroom, and immediately fell, landing primarily on my left knee. My wife woke up, turned on the light, and helped me climb (mainly using my arms) onto the bed. As I moved, I heard what

sounded like popcorn popping, but in reality, it was the sound of my left patella shattering. This is something I wouldn't know until about twelve hours later because I laid in bed until the sun came up and then asked Cristie to call for an ambulance. I was transported to the nearest emergency room that was affiliated with the hospital where I had outpatient PT and OT after moving to North Carolina but at that time was not physically attached to a hospital. Today, it's a women's hospital (it's not that they dislike men; they just don't care for them). Anyway, they took x-rays and told me my patella was in twenty-six pieces. They then proceeded to put my leg in a contraption called an immobilizer, which I thought sounded like the title of a bad Arnold Schwarzenegger movie (not that I've ever seen any really good ones). Next, they told me to see an orthopaedic surgeon as soon as possible and then discharged me. No crutches, no wheelchair, and, given that Cristie drives a Mini Cooper and I was donning the immobilizer that made my leg stick out straight, no ride home.

Later, my orthopaedic surgeon told me that they shouldn't have sent me home and that they should have transferred me to their main hospital facility for pain management and general care. So Cristie first tried to reach our pastor, who was a football player and big enough to help get me in the house, to see if he could come get me at the ER. Her second call was to my former physical therapist to try to wrangle a wheelchair. Both calls were successful. Once home, I basically lived on the living room sofa until I could get in to see the ortho doc. And it wasn't until a week after that (I had to get off my blood thinner) that the doctor humpty-dumptied my kneecap back together (versus knee replacement). Then it was back to physical therapy. But let me tell you something—if a mobster threatens to break your kneecap unless you come up with the cash, come up with the cash. A broken kneecap hurts big time! And, yes, I have fallen subsequent times since that fateful Saturday night. We get these tiny round acorns (larger than a BB pellet but smaller than a marble) every autumn, and they litter our driveway. They're not friends with either my feet or my cane. Throw rugs, freshly mopped floors and steep stairways present challenges, too. Since breaking the patella, I have refractured it, broken a few fingers and cracked a couple of ribs.

Do we really need gravity? I guess so. Otherwise, how would we know when a bird dies?

- *Fear of the unknown.* That's not exactly what my fear is, but I can't think of a more succinct way to express it. Let me give you an example. There's a recording studio I like to use that's in a restored historic building. The studios are on the second floor, and to get to them I have to climb a steep staircase that has a brick wall with no handrail on the right; and there's no elevator. This is tricky and probably a tad dangerous. I now tend to get anxious about going somewhere I've never been before or don't know what physical limitations might await me. And this can apply to anything from having to face a set of stairs with no handrail to a backyard barbecue at someone's home where I have to hold my plate, my glass and my cane—and heaven forbid it should get dark. Perhaps my true fear here is calling attention to myself, requiring my host to make special accommodations for me, or my having an accident (for Pete's sake, let's just call it falling) that requires medical attention. I have turned down several social invitations for this reason and have made arrangements to Skype meetings rather than physically attending. But I am getting better. Prior to going to a recording session for some radio commercials several months ago, I informed the producer that I'd had a stroke and had some physical limitations. And while I did have an issue with a set of stairs, everything else went fine. Having said that, I did turn down an invitation to a backyard celebration just a few weeks ago.
- *Fear of driving.* Because I drive using only my right hand, I use a Brodie knob, which is a ball that attaches to the steering wheel that spins and allows me to completely turn the steering wheel without needing my left hand. It's also known by the less fortunate name suicide knob. This dates back to the days of drag racing in the 1950s. A suicide knob allowed the daddy-Os to steer their dragsters with their left hands while having their right arms around the shoulders of their poodle-skirted, gum-popping baby dolls. Because of their bad-boy reputation, Brodie knobs are outlawed

in several states; however, my driver's license specifies that I can't drive without one. As a result, rental cars are off limits. By the way, my Brodie knob looks like a miniature basketball, which, if you know anything about North Carolina and collegiate sports, you know that my steering wheel accessory is quite apropos for where I reside.

I also used to drive a car with a manual transmission, but with only one good hand and a left leg that doesn't function like it should, I have to drive an automatic. This means I can't drive Cristie's Mini, which is more fun to drive than my SUV.

The fact I drive with only one hand does make me nervous at times. If someone were to suddenly cut me off, I just have my one good hand and my suicide knob to get me out of a jam. About two years ago, this happened in a fifty-five-mile-per-hour zone and, by some odd firing of neurons in my brain, my left hand grabbed the wheel, which was probably more dangerous. Having said that, there are some tall bridges I don't care to drive over on windy days simply because I'd prefer for someone with hands at ten and two (or is it now eight and four?) to do so.

I had to get permission from both a physician and my physical therapist before I could drive again. By this time, I was out of the wheelchair and walking with a cane. My aide drove me to the DMV, and when I went in, I had to go to this desk to get a number from the state trooper manning it. I thought it was interesting that the trooper immediately asked, "How long ago did you have your stroke?" I took the written (electronic) test and only got one thing wrong: I couldn't identify a school zone sign based solely on its shape (and I have since gotten a ticket for going too fast in a school zone). Then a female trooper and I went for a little ride in my newly Brodie knob-equipped SUV. I passed with flying colors. But when my aide and I got home, I joked with Cristie and told her I didn't pass. She replied, "I really didn't think they'd let you drive this soon after a stroke." When I showed her my new North Carolina license, she said she was happy for me but looked a bit nervous.

- *Fear of scaring my wife.* I'm certain that on February 4, 2006, I scared the crap out of Cristie. She has recounted on several occasions about how the female EMT gave her a hug to try to calm her down before climbing into the ambulance and taking me away. And to this day, the last thing I want to do is scare her like that again.

  However, I keep doing it. The night I fell and destroyed my patella, I frightened her big time. Several months ago I tripped in the bedroom, fell, and woke her up. I managed not to hurt myself, but I scared her so badly that she couldn't fall back to sleep for hours. Remember those mini-acorns I mentioned earlier? One evening Cristie was visiting family out of town. I went to take the dog out to the fenced-in portion of our backyard. Walking back into the house, I slipped on those little suckers, and while I didn't fall, I did wrench my back badly. When we talked on the phone later that night, she was scared I'd take a bad fall the next time.

  She also gets alarmed if she can't reach me by phone (house or cell) after a few hours. On more than one occasion after I didn't contact her, she left work and came home expecting to find me sprawled out on the floor. Now I try to do my best to let her know when I'm going out and call once I've returned.

  However, more times than not, when I call her during the day on her cell phone, I hear it ringing in the kitchen. Perhaps she leaves her phone at home because she doesn't want to be scared any more than I want to scare her.

- *Fear of another stroke.* I think anyone who has survived a stroke is lying if they say they have no fear of having another. According to the Centers for Disease Control and Prevention, approximately 185,000 people who survive a stroke go on to have another. The road to recovery is so long, so exhausting and so challenging that the mere thought of having to go through all of that again scares me more than anything on earth.

  Like I stated before, I didn't experience the typical symptoms most people have at the onset of my stroke. I didn't have the "I'll show you something worse than a migraine" headache, the blurred vision, or noticeable numbness. I merely felt sleepy. So today, if I suddenly get a bad headache, have problems reading something, or feel like the left side of my mouth is a little too droopy (as it does from time to time), I get nervous that number two is coming on.

But the truth is, my odds of having a second stroke are extremely small given the cornucopia of meds I take each day. I also exercise two to three times a week, watch what I eat, and regularly see my merry band of medical practitioners. But that doesn't stop that occasional uneasiness. I have a friend in Baltimore who had a wreck at a certain intersection years ago, and to this day, he goes to extreme measures to avoid that intersection. That's how I feel about the possibility of a second stroke. I will do whatever I can to avoid visiting the intersection of clot and cranium again.

Hi-Ho, Hi-Ho

In 1997, after nineteen years of working as a copywriter, group head and creative director at several advertising agencies, I decided to go off on my own and become a freelancer. I've been very fortunate in my career. I've worked for good people, learned from great mentors and been trusted with several opportunities that received honors. However, I was quite nervous about going out on my own, but I quickly found myself consistently busy with having to turn down a job here and there.

Most of my work came from various agencies, primarily in Richmond, Baltimore and DC. But I also got a couple of direct clients on my own, and at times I served as a creative consultant to companies looking to hire an agency or improve their relationship with their agency. On one occasion, an agency hired me to work there for six weeks to determine how they could improve their creative product. In 2004, I returned to the agency where I got my first job to work with an art director I had long admired. And I was finishing up a couple of projects for this shop when I had the stroke.

Like many industries, advertising people are a tight-knit, nearly incestuous little group of folks. So when word of my stroke broke, it spread through the ad community pretty quickly. And while it was fine that the phone wasn't ringing with job requests while I was recovering and rehabbing, jump-starting my career once I was well enough to get back to work proved tricky. Part of the problem was timing—2006 was the year the economy started to tank, and when corporations start tightening their belts, the first line item in the budget to get trimmed is marketing and advertising.

Plus I think many of my former clients were a bit gun-shy about calling me. Were they going to get the same old Andy, or had I dramatically changed? Would they have to treat me differently? Would I require special accommodations? Basically, was I damaged goods?

The other problem was I was now living in North Carolina, not that I needed to physically be at an agency in the era of Skype, FaceTime and such. However, plenty of agencies remain old school, and unless they see you on site, physically working on their behalf, they question whether they're actually getting their money's worth.

Initially, my sister gave me a few jobs promoting an open-air shopping mall she was working for. She had a marketing company called Ellis & Others, which was just her and other freelancers. Thanks to her many years in the shopping center industry and exceptional reputation, she knew great people she could call with equally strong experience. A client who is sort of my sister's equivalent, but in the world of economy hotel marketing, and with whom I've had an association for many years, had enough faith in me to send me work, but the phone wasn't ringing as much as I would have liked.

Following my sister's death in late 2006, I felt the need to sort of reinvent myself as a freelance entity. Borrowing from my late sister's business strategy, I launched Ellis & Others 2 in early 2007. To get the word out that I was available for work, I visited some old colleagues from my past in Atlanta and Baltimore. In the city of the Ravens and the Orioles, I visited an art director with whom I'd worked on several occasions and whom I like and admire as both an art director and a person. I got to the lobby of his agency, introduced myself to the receptionist, took a seat, and waited for Dave to escort me back to his office. After a couple of minutes, this young woman walked through the lobby, glancing once in my direction. Two beats later, she returned to the lobby, walked over to the receptionist and whispered, "Is that Andy Ellis?" The receptionist confirmed my identity, and the young woman, still whispering, said, "Are you sure? I heard he died."

Well, hell. No wonder the phone wasn't ringing. Who wants to work with a dead copywriter? They tend to smell after a while.

As a result, I made a point of establishing a presence on Facebook. I jumped (not literally, of course) at the chance to judge the Baltimore creative advertising awards a couple of years ago, and I'm diligent about sending out Christmas cards every year as evidence that I still walk this earth—albeit with a limp.

Things That Have Gone
the Way of the Dodo

Everyone knows and accepts the fact that, as they age, certain skills and abilities diminish and eventually become a topic that's preceded with the words "You know, there was a time when I loved [add the present participle of your choice]." This is traditionally a gradual occurrence. However, a stroke erases a wealth of aptitudes overnight. There are a number of skill sets I actually don't miss. For instance, I have no problem saying, "No, I can't clean out the gutters. I had a stroke and can't climb a ladder." And every day prior to the stroke I would think, *I'm one day closer to being able to say, "No I can't clean out the gutters because, at my age, I shouldn't climb a ladder."* I guess the joke's on me. But for every talent (and I say *talent* because—let me tell you—I was one *fine* gutter cleaner) I don't truly miss, there's another I lament losing. To some, the losses I grieve may seem trivial, but in some small way they made my life a little sweeter. Some readers might think, *What a flippin' whiner this Ellis guy is.* And I will agree to the extent that I am blessed and can do a lot of things many stroke survivors can't. I just miss these odd little things I used to take for granted.

- *Cutting the grass.* Who knows why this was the first thing that popped into my head, given I haven't mowed a lawn since we lived in Baltimore and that was in the 1990s. But we had a nice-size, fenced-in backyard that I groomed regularly in the spring and summer and could even create that Major League Baseball field diamond pattern in the grass in under an hour. For me, this was the definition of instant gratification. Of course, that "grass-related high" (not an intended pun) could be easily marred if I stepped in dog poop. Our front yard was a small, sloping hill covered in liriope (a.k.a. monkey grass or spider grass) that got trimmed once every spring with a weed eater. The yard we have now is much larger, and with only one totally functioning hand and arm and a rather defined limp, cutting the yard would take quite a while, and the result would probably not look anywhere close to the Major League quality of excellence I have established for myself. And while there was a riding mower in the garage when we inherited our current home, I doubt I'd get the same satisfaction of doing it by hand.

Since I mentioned dog poop that brings me to the second item on my miss list ...

- *Walking our dog.* When we lived in Baltimore, we got our first dog. While Cristie was reluctant about getting a dog, I'd had dogs in my life since I was eight. It was one Tuesday night in February 1992, while watching the "working dog group" at the Westminster Kennel Club show on *USA* when a large, white dog entered the ring, and my wife casually said, "There's a dog I could like." A few short months later, we went to a small town in Pennsylvania and returned with a Great Pyrenees pup we named Beth. Primarily used in mountainous regions to guard flock, these gentle giants range from twenty-five to thirty-six inches at the shoulders. Once fully grown, Beth was closer to the thirty-six-inch end. She was a big girl who was kind of a portable petting zoo. People were constantly coming up to us asking to pet her, and she loved being loved. In fact, she'd frequently pull to get closer to people in hopes they'd pet her. While I understand a dog that size might intimidate someone, she could not have been a sweeter dog. I would always take her on her morning walks and, once I became self-employed, her evening walks as well. And I truly enjoyed it.

There was a park near our house called Sherwood Gardens that was the size of a city block, and this was the destination of our evening walks. On one occasion, a man with two small children was in the park. Upon seeing Beth, he started moving his children away from us. Now, as I mentioned, Beth was prone to pulling to get to people in hopes of being loved, but seeing how this dad was instilling the fear of God in his children over my dog (I firmly believe in teaching children to respect animals but not to fear them without just cause), I tried to steer clear. However, eventually our paths did cross, and when the father asked, "Does your dog like children?" I casually replied, "Yes, but they spoil her appetite." I don't recall ever seeing that man or his kids in Sherwood Gardens again. Beth has since crossed the Rainbow Bridge (Google it if you don't know what I'm talking about), but now we have another Pyr from the same lineage, a male named Surge Protector (he came with this name), or Surge for short. These are large, strong animals. There were times walking Beth when she'd see a cat half a city block ahead and want to take off after it (she liked to play with cats, not hurt them), nearly pulling my arm out of its socket. Now that I walk with a cane using my right hand and have partial paralysis in my left arm, I'm no longer a good candidate for walking such a large animal. I've had people ask on numerous occasions why we got such large dogs, and my standard answer is, "I'm just too lazy to bend over to love my pet." Now my wife walks Surge twice a day, and I'm jealous. I miss those times.

- *Driving a manual transmission.* If my father were still alive, he'd tell you that learning to drive with a stick shift didn't come naturally or quickly to me. However, once I got it down, I didn't want to give it up. My last manual transmission car was a Toyota Celica, and it was flat-out fun to drive. We bought our first automatic transmission car shortly after we got Beth and realized a 125-pound dog didn't fit too well in a sports car. So we got a Jeep Grand Cherokee with a six-speed automatic. We now have a Toyota FJ Cruiser, which I drive and Cristie hates; I will admit it does have serious blind spots. But she drives a Mini Cooper with a manual transmission. When I drove her car (pre-stroke), it was all kinds of fun. It was like driving a go-kart on steroids. Now the best I can do is get it in and out of the garage. My left leg can't work the clutch very well, and shifting gears means taking my one good hand off the steering wheel—not a plan my insurance company really likes.

- *Pushing my son's wheelchair.* This is very similar to not being able to cut the grass. I believe my son got his first actual wheelchair when he was around age four or five, and I enjoyed taking him places. I've never appreciated the term *wheelchair bound* as it implies the person is a prisoner of the wheelchair. The newer, perhaps more appropriate phrase is *wheelchair enabled*, implying that a person who cannot walk can still get around and take in all life has to offer. And to an extent, a wheelchair frequently treats its occupant to perks. I can't tell you how many times Graham and his chair managed to get him to the front of the line everywhere from the National Aquarium and Disney World to a ballpark and the next spot to visit Santa. When I'd take Graham out, I was often surprised by how many people knew him. His public school system (Chesterfield County, Virginia, Public School System) did an amazing, highly progressive job of integrating special needs students with the general student population. So when Graham and I would go to the grocery store near his mom's house (post-divorce), we'd frequently be greeted by several people saying, "Hey, Graham." I've always felt that Graham has a kind of ministry that teaches people it's okay to look at someone in a wheelchair. Today, Graham is thirty and lives in a group home in a rural area of Virginia. His current wheelchair is rather elaborate and way too heavy for me to push and steer with one hand. While I can still go see him at the group home, we are limited as to where we can go. I just miss our little outings.
- *Playing guitar.* I started playing guitar around age twelve. And while I was never really accomplished at the instrument, I did enjoy playing and occasionally writing a song. I also played bass guitar from time to time. Even prior to the stroke, I was playing less frequently. I blamed this on pride. I've written and produced hundreds and hundreds of radio and TV commercials with original music composed specifically for that ad. I've spent a good bit of time in recording studios with highly talented musicians, singers, and composers, including a few truly, truly talented guitarists. The two who immediately come to mind are Velpo Robertson in Richmond and Wall Mathews in Baltimore. After spending even

the least amount of time around these gentlemen, going home and playing the same instrument myself was a sheer disappointment. I had an electric Gibson that hadn't been out of its case in ages, so I gave it to a friend in Baltimore who I knew would play and enjoy it. However, I kept my acoustic and continued to play it infrequently—until the stroke. Now the fingers on my left hand have very little dexterity and, as I've stated before, it's hard for me to control how much pressure these fingers can and can't apply.

So here comes a sweet story: I have this thing about owning something and not putting it to its use. By this I usually mean a tool or something that has a purpose. I don't know where this came from, but it's the reason I gave the electric guitar to my friend. It bothered me that this well-crafted instrument was merely residing in a hard plastic case when it was intended to make music. Fast-forward to post-stroke in North Carolina. An aide to my physical therapist who is a pretty good guitar player learned I had a guitar and, for my birthday, restrung it and gave me a glass bottleneck slide. His aim was to get me to play the guitar as occupational therapy. While I'll admit I probably didn't give it enough effort or patience, I found myself getting frustrated and pissed off with every attempt. I do, however, greatly appreciate my friend trying to help me. Now again fast-forward to September 2012, aboard Holland America Line's *Ms Zaandam* cruising Alaska. Prior to dinner, most nights, we'd go to the Ocean Bar for wine. And every evening, we were waited on by a kind, young Filipino gentleman named Jonathan. The Ocean Bar was also home to a jazz quartet of piano, bass, drums and guitar. Like many of the crew aboard cruise ships, waiting tables at the Ocean Bar in the evening wasn't Jonathan's only job. He probably had a job during the morning and afternoon in some other capacity in food and beverage. Well, one particular evening, Jonathan greeted us with his customary, "So how was your day?" We recounted whatever wonderful experience we'd had since last seeing him, and I always felt a little guilty because while we were on vacation, he was at work serving people who were on vacation. However, this particular evening when I asked Jonathan how his day was, he told us he'd had the day off. Cristie asked him how he'd spent the day. He replied, "Like I do every day off. I went to pawn shops in town looking for a guitar I can afford to buy." At dinner that night, I suggested to my wife that we give Jonathan my guitar. The next evening, I asked Jonathan to write down all the information I'd need if I wanted to send him a letter or a package. It turns out these crew members get mail very infrequently.

Once home, I got in touch with our Holland America agent in Seattle and learned when the *Ms Zaandam* would be docked in San Diego and exactly how to ship a package (a large package, mind you) to Jonathan. So off to Ship-On-Site I went with my guitar and a guitar case that had seen better days. There I said good-bye to my beautiful instrument, and ten days later I received an e-mail from the dock master saying my package had arrived and he'd get it to Jonathan once the ship docked. It was about a month later when I received an e-mail with a photo attached of a smiling Jonathan in his tiny cabin holding his new guitar. Every now and then, I look at that picture and it makes me very happy. If I can't play it, I'm happy knowing that Jonathan can.

• *Mouth stuff.* I know this is going to seem strange, and I know it's *my* hang-up and that very few people can see or notice that the left side of my mouth droops. My beard and mustache probably hide it pretty well from the rest of the world, but I can see it and I know what it affects. On what I call my "off days" or when I'm tired, I am likely to slightly drool, especially while speaking. My neurologist has given me several mouth-related exercises, which she suggests I do in front of a mirror. This is when I'm hyperaware of the droopiness. These exercises range from quickly pursing my lips over and over to repeating "Here, kitty, kitty, kitty" as rapidly and as many times as I can. The funny thing is my neurologist had a great physician's assistant for a while whose name was Kitty. I read somewhere about another exercise where you lip-sync songs while looking in a mirror. I find this exercise very frustrating because it looks like I'm the world's worst lip-syncer.

Beyond the occasional drooling episode and an inability to mouth the words to "Bohemian Rhapsody," I can no longer whistle, sing, or entertain small children. Okay, let me explain. I can't form my lips to whistle like I could before. The singing issue (not that I was that great of a singer before but, again, give me a gutter clogged with leaves, and stand back) is a combination of my mouth problems and lacking lung-capacity control. This is also the reason I frequently run out of air midsentence, sometimes causing me to talk too fast, which leads to people not understanding what I'm trying to say. As far as entertaining children, pre-stroke I could do a spot-on Donald Duck imitation and a pretty funny chicken imitation, but, alas, today I can no longer delight children with poultry noises.

And then there's my general speaking voice. As I mentioned, I have issues with lung capacity and tend to talk quickly, so I have to stop midsentence to get another ration of oxygen. My neurologist has strongly advised me to purposefully speak slower because I live in North Carolina and don't have a southern accent. She said she has to speak slower to southerners because of her Oklahoma upbringing and total lack of an accent. The timbre of my voice has dramatically changed. My voice has a considerably higher pitch to it. I don't know if my vocal cords have been altered or what. I spoke with someone a few months ago I hadn't spoken to since well before the stroke. I mentioned that she sounded exactly like she used to, and she replied that I sounded nothing like I used to. I hate hearing my voice now on voice mail or a playback at a recording session. In college, I was the manager of the student radio station, and I did a morning show and worked as a disc jockey for a while following graduation. So I had a fairly decent set of pipes on me. I'm certain that no longer smoking has erased a richer huskiness to my voice as well.

Typing with two hands. It's true. Every word you're reading here was typed with one hand as typing with my left hand would require too much effort, thought and concentration to hit one specific key. Initially following the stroke, I invested in speech-recognition software. Now this was nearly a decade ago, and this technology has made major strides and my speech has improved to an extent. But back then the only value of such software (at least for me) was for entertainment purposes. At times, it was hysterical to read what the application thought I was trying to say. For example, a line from a radio commercial I wrote around this time that was supposed to read "Shop Local Day, April 27th, is an initiative between the Lancaster by the Bay Chamber and Chesapeake Bank," would come out as something like, "Stop logical Dave, April heaven his institute the knees the forecaster by-and-by chancellor of chess piece plank." It was like some really bad translation from a foreign language. I now wish I'd saved some of these documents it created (I don't want to name the application) because many were *so* far off from what I thought I'd actually said it was hysterical. So I resorted to one-hand typing, but the biggest problem there was that by the time I was halfway through typing a sentence, I'd frequently forget exactly how I wanted to convey a particular thought. But with time and practice, I'm now up to about forty-four words a minute with only my right hand. It isn't pretty, but it works.

That's pretty much true for all post-stroke adaptations. As with the frustrations and fears I discussed previously, every stroke survivor will find his or her unique way to skin his or her own cats (an expression I've never understood and don't want to Google fearing they'll show me a photograph I won't be able to unsee).

You Have Got to Be Effing Kidding Me

R ight off the bat, I fear this chapter might come off as either preachy or braggadocio. Neither is intended. This is just some news I discovered that surprised me.

I found a newspaper article written by Tara Kulash of the *St. Louis Post-Dispatch* headlined "Many Stroke, Heart-Attack Survivors Fail to Change Lifestyle." My first thought was, *I had to have misread that.* My second was, *Am I reading* The National Examiner *or* The Globe?

But the article quotes a study from April 2013 by the American Medical Association that shows one in four men doesn't make any lifestyle change following a heart attack, stroke, or other cardiac event. Three behaviors were included for this study: smoking cessation, healthy eating, and physical exercise. Of the seven-thousand-plus patients surveyed in seventeen countries, just 4.3 percent of participants improved their habits in all three areas. Some 30 percent made two lifestyle changes, and 47 percent changed only one lifestyle behavior to better their health.

In her article, Kulash cites lack of education as the reason behind these sad statistics. Quoting from the article, "While patients used to stay in the hospital for up to two weeks after a cardiac event, they now are discharged within a day or two. This leaves little time for the medical staff to educate patients on what happened to them and what it could mean for their future."

So, in a manner of speaking, I was blessed to have stayed in the hospital for over fifty days because I received quite an education on the causes of and ways to prevent a stroke. The speech pathologist hosted a weeklong class that all in-patient stroke survivors were required to attend. Each session was about thirty minutes and covered the same topics the AMA study examined. Since my stay at Henrico Doctors' was prolonged, I took this course a good five times.

Seriously, I thought the pathologist would have graduated me after taking the course twice. But, no. In fact, she kept me on as sort of a shill. By that, I mean following the lessons, she'd quiz us, and if someone answered a question incorrectly, she'd turn to me and say (in a somewhat demeaning manner), "Andy, will you please tell (insert embarrassed patient's name here) what the correct answer is?" While this made me, more or less, the teacher's pet, it didn't endear me to my fellow stroke survivors. And on more than one occasion, she'd ask an African American patient what race has the largest percentage of deaths from strokes and why. When the poor patient couldn't answer the question, again the pathologist would ask, "Andy, will you please tell (insert embarrassed black patient's name here) what the correct answer is?" I'd truthfully respond as the pathologist had taught (and the American Stroke Association website bears out), "African Americans have a much higher risk of death from a stroke than Caucasians, partially because Blacks have higher risks of high blood pressure, diabetes, and obesity." So not only did I feel like the teacher's pet, but I also felt a bit like the class bigot.

Perhaps the most surprising and most optimistic fact to emerge from this study was that 52 percent of stroke survivors kicked the cigarette habit. Many, many times prior to my stroke, if people had asked me what one thing I would change about my life if I could go back in time, the answer would definitely have been that I would never have taken up smoking. But I will admit—I did enjoy it.

While giving up cigarettes wasn't a cakewalk, I had two things going for me. I was on a smoking cessation patch that was correctly administered to me by my nurses. Plus I had an oxygen tube in my nose that would have exploded if I'd lit up. (It happened on an episode of *Grey's Anatomy*, so it must be true.) I had tried several times prior to the stroke to quit smoking but failed every time. But my physicians in the hospital made it abundantly clear to me that smoking had played a major role in my stroke, so the odds of my ever lighting up again are infinitesimal.

My parents were smokers, with my mother smoking up to the day she passed away. While Mom didn't die directly as a result of her habit, it did diminish her health and led to a heart valve replacement on April 19, 1995. The only reason I know the date is because her surgery was on the same day as the Oklahoma City bombing. And two days later when she finally woke up in her hospital room, my father and I were watching CNN at the foot of her bed with our backs to my mom. Suddenly she came to, saw the television, and said, "What the hell happened?"

Anyway, I digress. The point is the last cigarette I had, and will ever have, is the one Cristie took out of my hand while I was having the stroke. Today, even the smell of cigarette smoke makes me feel ill. I think I was lucky that I got to quit in what could be considered a rehab environment. I have a dear friend who has tried absolutely every cessation therapy available (gum, patch, prescription, etc.) to no avail. He even said he had come up with his own cessation program—every time he wanted a cigarette, he'd masturbate. The downside, he said, was, "I'd probably pass out by 9:30 a.m." Today, he has severe emphysema and lung cancer.

So if my mom is looking down on me from heaven thinking I hath more virtue than a reformed whore, then so be it. I can't imagine someone continuing to smoke following a cardiac event.

But wait. I'm not ready to get off my soapbox quite yet.

In addition to giving up cigarettes, I have also improved my eating habits. I wasn't a horrible eater before, but before the day of my stroke became yesterday, it was determined that my cholesterol level was well over 200.

Once I was able to return to the kitchen, more fish and poultry recipes were added to my repertoire. I seriously endorse *The American Heart Association Cookbook*. I've also learned to swap out things in recipes (for example, 2 percent milk instead of cream really makes very little difference in terms of taste). So, again, I can't understand why someone who survived a cardiac event wouldn't modify his or her eating habits.

And while I am eating far healthier than I did pre-stroke, I am overweight. This is primarily due to the fact that I am less physically active on a day-to-day basis—meaning, I can't walk any significant distance and my pace is pretty slow.

This brings us to the third behavior examined in the AMA study: physical exercise.

I consider myself blessed that two weeks following the stroke, I started physical and occupational therapies at Henrico Doctors'. The therapy room resembled a regular gym with a lot of the same fitness equipment. Therapy started each weekday shortly after breakfast and usually kicked off with a ten-minute warm-up on the chest press or a rowing machine (I assume this was to build upper-body strength for the day when the patient is introduced to their walker). Midmorning, I'd switch from physical therapy to occupational therapy. While I loved both of my therapists, I found OT to be far more frustrating. Most of the fine motor skills associated with my left hand were shot, plus I'd lost a great deal of sensitivity in my fingers. Hence, picking up small pegs and placing them in equally small holes on a board was difficult and frequently swear-worthy. But my dear, sweet, twenty-two-year-old therapist was patient, encouraging and unrelenting, which is something they must teach at therapy school. Hers was the first face I'd see every morning as she came to my room with her cup of coffee to help me get dressed.

I recall one day when a new patient, who I believe was rehabbing from an automobile accident rather than a stroke, was wheeled into the therapy room. I was with my PT at the time, and my OT was tending to this new patient, who was being belligerent, raising his voice to my OT and saying he wasn't going to do therapy and she couldn't make him. I think a fatherly instinct kicked in inside me when he started to swear at her, as I wanted to go over and inform this asshole that he was indeed being an asshole. By the same token, I was confused as to why someone who was being offered the chance to get better would refuse it. Finally, my OT—my dear, sweet, twenty-two-year-old therapist—told the guy, "I can't make you do therapy, and you have the right to refuse it, but I'm not wheeling you back to your room." And there he sat in his wheelchair while the rest of us went on with the work of rehab. If I could have gotten to my feet, I would have given her a standing ovation.

Around noon, we'd break for lunch, which also included those stroke education classes I mentioned earlier. Then it was back to therapy until around five o'clock. In her book *My Stroke of Insight*, neuroanatomist Dr. Jill Bolte Taylor states that following her stroke in 1996 at age thirty-seven, she had little therapy and instead rested a great deal. I have no idea if one treatment is better than another, but I do know that when 5:00 p.m. rolled around each weekday, I was ready to rest.

There was also in-patient therapy on the weekends, but it was abridged and was with whatever therapist drew the short straw for that weekend (that's not true—it was a rotating schedule). Of the forty-plus days I had therapy, I missed only one session and that was on a Sunday because I had some sort of twenty-four-hour stomach bug. In fact, I was Mr. Perfect Attendance at outpatient therapy at HealthSouth Rehab in Richmond following my hospital stay, as well as at WakeMed Outpatient Rehab in Raleigh after moving to North Carolina. Mind you, it doesn't hurt that, statistically, therapists tend to be attractive, physically fit, young women. But my true motivation for not missing therapy was my desire to get better. I honestly thought that if I worked hard enough and long enough, I'd be 100 percent back to the way I was pre-stroke. I guess one thing the speech pathologist forgot to teach in the stroke education class was that this rarely, rarely happens. But here it is ten years down the road, and I haven't given up. I periodically revisit or try new things to see if they might help even a little.

At a doctor's suggestion (I can't remember which one, probably my neurologist), I tried Botox injections in my left arm to reduce spasticity. Was it painful? Yes. Did it work? Not really. However, in defense of this treatment, my son was receiving injections in his arms to reduce spasticity and it did help.

Also with an introduction from one of my wife's coworkers, I met Rosemary Herlong, who is considered to be one of the leading aquatic therapists in the United States. And she just happened to live near Raleigh and was willing to take me on as a patient on Saturday mornings. While we first did therapy at a really old, fairly sketchy-looking indoor pool at a deteriorating YWCA, we soon switched to Gypsy Divers, a large indoor swimming facility primarily used to teach scuba diving. The deep end of this pool is twelve-feet deep, and frequently I would be swimming on the surface while several scuba divers were doing their thing several feet below me. From the surface they looked like manatees. I recall early on in aquatic therapy when the therapist asked if I could tread water. When I was a teenager, I got Red Cross certified as a lifeguard, so in my head I was thinking, *Sure, I know how to tread water.* But in truth, my post-stroke body *didn't* know how to tread water, and I quickly sunk. Within a couple of months, however, I was doing backstroke laps up and down the pool. Later on, my therapist made up a volleyball-like game where we'd bat this beach ball back and forth to each other in about five-feet-deep water.

This was a good workout on several levels. First, Rosie would tell me which hand to use to bat the ball, causing me to use my left arm and hand. Plus, any exercise in water takes double the strength it would on land, making this a pretty exhausting workout. After telling me one of her former patients had passed away that week, Rosie informed me that she'd never had an active (existing) patient die, to which I responded, "Then I guess you're stuck with me forever." About a year later, she moved to Wilmington. When she told me we'd be ending our therapy sessions, I joked, "Does this mean I'm going to die?" And to this day, I occasionally e-mail her to say, "Nice try, but I'm still alive." I highly endorse aquatic therapy or any type of water exercise. The Rex Wellness Center, an exercise facility my wife and I belong to that's ten minutes from our house and is affiliated with a major hospital in Raleigh, offers an aquatic range-of-motion class a couple times a week, and I always feel a bit more nimble after taking the class.

While I was officially graduated from physical and occupational therapies in 2007, I have returned to both for a booster shot. As I mentioned before, there was an incident where a driver suddenly cut me off, and my left hand, which normally rests on my left thigh while I drive, grabbed the steering wheel. While this was probably more dangerous than helpful, it did indicate that at least one neuron path I thought terminated was somewhat still open for business. I contacted my neurologist and told her this story, and she wrote me a script to return to occupational therapy. I found a great therapist, and while we worked diligently twice a week for about three months, all that really came of it was a slight increase in hand strength. I'm still safer driving with the Brodie knob than getting my left hand involved. But the point is there was a glimmer of a possibility that I could regain greater use of my left hand, and I jumped on the opportunity to find out. Similarly, when I saw my neurologist last autumn, she noticed I had some increased spasticity in my left arm and leg. Hence, she wrote a prescription to reduce hypertonicity and another for PT. Both proved helpful. I credit the physical therapy and my therapist for picking up the pace of my walking, improving my balance, and making me less susceptible to falling.

Fortune also shone down on me when the former aide to one of my physical therapists started working as a personal trainer at the wellness center. This means that someone who is abundantly aware of my physical deficits and has an understanding of where and how I can overcome some of my issues is directing my exercise program.

My point here is I personally can't understand or imagine *not* making all three of the lifestyle changes investigated in the AMA study. I will admit that it's not always easy, and I am certainly no superman for making the changes I made. While I'm certainly not 100 percent back to where I was pre-stroke, most of my doctors and therapists are surprised by how much I have regained. And the fact of the matter is that I've worked my ass off to come this far, and the last thing I can imagine is having to start all over again following a second stroke. I've told my wife that if I have another stroke, please just push me off the sofa and let me die on the floor. I can't do this again. But this request comes with the responsibility to do everything in my power to not have another stroke. I will continue to seek ways to get better, stronger and healthier. I owe that to my wife; the people who saved my life; the good people who've invested a great deal of time, energy and talent in my recovery; and *myself.*

When I was preparing to leave the hospital, somebody (I can't recall if it was my neurologist or one of my therapists, but it was someone I trusted) said to me, "What you get back six months after the stroke is about all you'll ever regain." I'm here to proclaim that statement is sheer bullshit. These days, I may regain only one or two things a year, and they may be fairly insignificant, but I regained something, right?

And I'm not going to effing quit.

Four Tips to Lower the Risk of a Second Stroke

Now that I've gone off about not making lifestyle changes, perhaps it would only be responsible of me to explain what can be done to reduce one's risk for a stroke. So allow me to share the four steps the National Stroke Association suggests.

1. *Eat Fruits and Vegetables.* The NSA recommends the Mediterranean or DASH (Dietary Approaches to Stop Hypertension) diets, which are rich in fruits, vegetables and whole grains.

2. *Know Your Digits.* Optimal blood pressure is 120 over 80. Optimal cholesterol is below 200 mg/dL (milligrams per deciliter), and optimal blood sugar is below 5.7 percent. Obviously, this involves getting an annual physical complete with blood work. I get mine every April from my internist. He also checks out my overall health, including a prostate exam that comes with the same joke every year—"If you'd like a second opinion, I can use two fingers."

3. *Eat Smaller Portions.* Most restaurants serve portions equal to three to five healthy servings. There are two Mexican restaurants near us. One I think firmly believes that if you clean your plate and can actually stand and walk out of the joint, they haven't done their job. The other serves three small (five-inch round) soft tacos with such ingredients as fresh fish, pineapple, grilled chicken, grilled steak, and veggies, and they don't slather everything in cheese or sour cream, and I always leave there sated but never stuffed. The National Stroke Association suggests asking for a to-go box and putting half of your meal in it before you start eating. Eat slower

because it takes time for your stomach to tell your brain you're full. Lower your sodium (salt) intake to 2,300 mg a day. I love soups and most people consider them to be healthy, but most canned and restaurant soups are loaded with salt.

4. *Participate in Physical Activity.* Aim for forty minutes per day, three to four times a week. If you can't do forty minutes, break it into four ten-minute workouts. For moderate exercise, try brisk walking, tennis, gardening or mopping the floors. I belong to a wellness center and try to work out three times a week, usually starting with a cardio warm-up followed by the circuit machines to strengthen knees and hips, then upper body strength, and ending with stretches. I frequently see a group of four men at the wellness center who are around my age, possibly a little older. But one guy in the group, sort of the ringleader, I rarely see actually exercising. Instead, I see him seated on the chest-press machine with the other three gentlemen standing around as this guy holds court talking about sports and politics. I've given up waiting to use the machine at times as that guy just sat there exercising his jaw. What cracks me up is that he always has a towel around his neck but doesn't sweat a single bead. And I'm sure he tells his doctor, "Oh, yeah, doc, I go to the gym four days a week."

For anyone with an ounce of common sense, these tips are obvious. In fact, I'm kind of surprised they didn't include, "Don't stick your tongue in an electrical outlet."

CHUNK #3

BEING DEFEATED IS OFTEN A TEMPORARY CONDITION—GIVING UP IS WHAT MAKES IT PERMANENT

How It All Looked from the Other Side of the Bed - by Cristie Dowda

I was not even supposed to be in Ashland the day my husband had his stroke. The first inkling was a Donald Duck voice. My back was toward him, and when I turned to see why he was humoring me with this not-entirely-unusual imitation, I froze. I just stared at him as he continued to babble in an indistinguishable fashion. The left side of his face looked like a Salvador Dali painting. In fact, the entire left side of his body seemed paralyzed while he remained completely oblivious, gamely puffing away on a cigarette in his right hand. One Mississippi, two Mississippi, and finally the realization hit that he was having a massive stroke.

There is nothing like a near-death experience to affirm the depth of your love for someone. As I frantically tried to keep my husband awake while clutching the handheld phone—my lifeline to the 911 operator—all I could think was, *Please, God, don't let this man die.* The kind voice instructed me and stayed on the phone until the ambulance arrived. It seemed like forever.

The EMT team asked questions, including which of the two equidistant hospitals I preferred, quickly ascertained the situation, strapped my husband onto a wheeled gurney, and were out the door. I stood in the emptied room and sobbed. While the two men put Andy in the ambulance, an intuitive and caring woman came back into the cottage. She hugged me and calmly advised that I would not be able to see my husband right away at the hospital. She said to take time to collect myself and make some phone calls. To this day, I am grateful for people I was never able to properly thank.

Nevertheless, I immediately left two messages for my son who lived nearby, grabbed my purse, and rushed to the hospital to, indeed, sit in the waiting room. Hearing two phones ring in rapid succession alerted my son, who happens to be a pastor, to a potential problem, and unbeknownst to me he started on his way—albeit to the wrong location. Perhaps I should have taken a bit longer to collect myself because I had failed to mention we were not at Henrico's main hospital.

The waiting room soon lost its charm, and I went outside to call my son again. I remember punching numbers on the cell phone but stopped when I heard "Mom" and saw him racing across the parking lot. The image is burned in my brain, and I remember feeling immediate relief. What a comfort to have someone who loves you in the sterile environment of a hospital. That would be my new reality. In a nanosecond, your life focus shifts. There is no preparation for trauma; you are thrown into it, and you flounder to survive. But you do.

In a short period of time, I had learned three important truths: it's important to be knowledgeable about the best medical facilities in your area, heed the advice of medical professionals and seek the care and support of family and friends.

Now, I was about to get a crash course in stroke. At that time, the harsh reality was that little could be done, medically speaking, to treat a stroke once activated. When we were finally able to see Andy in the ER, he was lying there with his eyes open, but nobody was home. I thought it was possible he could just slip away. It felt unreal. All the stark images are jumbled in my mind. The neurologist on call entered the picture and informed me of a drug that could be administered within the first three hours to help diminish the stroke impact, but there were side effects. Great, what are the other options? None. Okay, then, administer away.

We were moved to a holding area before being transferred to a high-care unit on the second floor. By then, it was evening, and the only room available was shared. I was absolutely torn apart when it became necessary to leave for the night. Everything in my being wanted to stay by my husband's side. He was so vulnerable, and the thought of leaving him alone was heartbreaking. I left his room and broke down in the hallway. Jewell, a nurse's aide, comforted me and assured me that she would find a private room so I could stay the next night.

She was true to her word. When I arrived early the next morning, a Sunday, we moved. I made some calls to family and close friends. News travels fast—the more tragic it is, the faster it goes, it seems. My first phone call was from the president of the seminary where I work as a grant writer. He told me that everyone at the seminary loved us and was praying for us. He said I was exactly where I needed to be and should stay there as long as it took. The assurance and peace I received calmed me. It was February; I would not return to work full-time until August.

Now, I understand that kind of latitude is not possible for everyone. But I count it an immense blessing to have been able to love and encourage my husband through one of the darkest periods of his life. From the outset, the neurologist assured me Andy would get better, that he would come back. For months, every time the poor man arrived, I beleaguered him to repeat those words to me. I needed to believe it.

While deep and abiding love is necessary to sustain your strength in a traumatic situation, you'll also be called to be an advocate. As medical consumers, we have the right to be informed and to make decisions. It may be necessary to intervene when medical needs are not being met and to fight for what you know is right. And if you are not around at dawn's first light when the doctors make their rounds before going to their offices, everything about your loved one's care will be secondhand information. You will not be able to ask questions or hear the encouragement you need to survive. While it is important not to be a hindrance to the steady stream of medical professionals coming into the room, being there is an education as you learn what treatments are being provided and for what purpose. This knowledge can ease the transition to home.

While I am not certain exactly how long it was before Andy began to verbally communicate with clarity, I think it was at least a week. Not surprisingly, his first thoughts were to find humor. For the next two weeks, I stayed in the hospital room and semi-slept in an upright chair at night. Countless friends streamed in and out, providing a balm to our weary spirits. Everyone needs a break; mine was leaving for a few hours to exercise.

People who love you will offer to help. Say yes to the friend who wants to bring you clothes because you only have a weekend's worth. Let someone else do your laundry, bring you some hot soup from Joe's Market, or smuggle in a Mason jar of white wine. When neighbors are coming through the area, let them bring your amassed mail and a few necessities from home. Thank those who offer tech support, setting up a blog or fixing the broken computer in Andy's office. In the same vein as you desire to help people you love, they are blessed to do the same for you. Target your requests to their strengths. When my sister-in-law implored me to give her something to do, I asked her to ascertain the best specialists in the Raleigh-Durham area in preparation for future care. As a well-connected public relations professional, there was no better person suited to the task, and those doctors, save one, remain Andy's care providers today.

After two weeks, Andy was ready for rehab and transferred to the fourth floor. I requested to stay the first night for the transition but understood that what my husband really needed was to regain his independence. The therapists poured themselves into their work, challenging and encouraging him every step of the way. These individuals are the real heroes in my husband's physical recovery. My regard for the nursing staff is equally positive, except for one instance. There was an RN who had a thinly veiled disgust either for weakness or my husband in particular. Whether it was her military background or a call to the wrong profession, I am unsure. Protocol to ensure safety required hospital personnel to be present whenever Andy needed to get out of bed. One evening, she refused to answer his third call for assistance even though she was not busy with another patient. The next day, I went to the head nurse, explained the sequence of events, and insisted that this person never be assigned to his "care" again. I remember asking, "Should my husband be subjected to the further indignity of wetting his bed?"

The most important advice I can give is to know the symptoms of stroke and act on them. In hindsight, I believe Andy had a series of transient ischemic attacks (TIAs)—basically mini strokes—that went undetected. At the time, we were living in different states. I now recall hearing garbled speech during telephone conversations and asking him what in the world was going on. In retrospect, it sounded eerily similar to that Donald Duck voice. If you even think you are experiencing symptoms of a TIA, seek medical attention immediately.

Humor. Fortitude. Determination. Perseverance. Humor. These are the qualities my husband exhibited through months of in-hospital therapy. We celebrated each new achievement together. He stayed the course and continues to amaze me with his resilience.

There have been some trying times post-stroke. In November 2007, we had just gotten past the need for a wheelchair when Andy fell coming to bed one evening. He has a high threshold for pain, so I had no idea of the severity until the next morning. He needed medical attention and could not walk, so I called 911. In this particular incidence, I completely failed as a medical advocate. I could just claim I was shell-shocked. But the reality is after he arrived via ambulance, I allowed the local ER to discharge Andy in a knee-immobilizer when he clearly should have been admitted to a hospital—gross incompetence, including mine. I should add that my car is a Mini, we no longer had a wheelchair at home, and there is no way a five-foot, six-inch average-sized woman can tote a man into the house. All I could think to do was to call the pastor of the church we had recently started attending and ask him for help. James Roberson III rescued us. Thankfully, he is also a big, buff guy who played college football a few years back. He drove his compact sedan to the ER, put Andy into the passenger seat, carried him into our house, and placed him on the sofa, where he stayed for several days before we could see a knee specialist. In the interim, we borrowed a wheelchair from his therapist. The upshot was that Andy had shattered his patella and would require surgery, returning him to a wheelchair for months. That night, I walked our dog, Surge, down our tree-lined street, sobbing the entire way. The unfairness of it broke my heart for him, and probably for me too. But, again, Andy persevered.

In a matter of days, a friend and skilled contractor designed and built a heavy-duty wooden wheelchair ramp in two sections so it could be disassembled and stored for future use. Our home occupational therapist was mightily impressed. However, at the time, we did not fully appreciate the ingenuity of this design.

I am convinced if you empower people with the ability to do something good, they will respond. In fact, a recent NBC News online poll found that nine in ten of us say being kind to others makes us happier than having others be kind to us. Following Andy's knee surgery, he was in an immobilizer and back in the chair. We were a few weeks away from a planned two-week vacation at the Outer Banks in an ocean-front home without an elevator. Of course, we had not purchased travel insurance. In desperation, or possibly brilliance, I refused to go down without a fight and wrote a no-holds-barred impassioned plea. I explained how my husband had been vacationing in the Outer Banks since he was two, that he was a stroke survivor and this was our annual vacation, but he was now confined to a wheelchair again. Would it be possible to make a generous contribution to the local fire department to carry my husband and his chair to the top floor? Was there anything that could be done? I faxed it to the real estate rental office and followed up with a phone call. Lo and behold, the office manager said she would make it happen. Two men from the realtor carried Andy up when we arrived and down two weeks later. I admit it was kind of scary, and my sweet husband had to stay put for the entire vacation. But he did have a great ocean view.

Periodically, Andy will refer to his "Andicapped" parking and say, "Aren't you glad I had a stroke?" Of course not, but through the ordeal we have grown closer. Sometimes he will apologize for his health issues, saying, "You didn't sign onto this." But actually I did. When I vowed to love and cherish in sickness and in health, I meant it. I tell him it could be me.

There could be a freak accident or some hidden genetic Molotov cocktail ready to explode.

Adversity strengthens us. When Jesus was on earth, He taught us to pray, "Give us this day our daily bread." We are to live in the present one day at a time. God did not promise a problem-free life; He promised to be ever-present, and I can testify that in the tough times, His presence is the only thing that can sustain. When people commented about how wonderfully I was enduring everything, I was quick to point to the One responsible for it all.

> Because of the Lord's great love we are not consumed, for his compassions never fail. They are new every morning; great is your faithfulness. (Lamentations 3:22–23)

> Be anxious for nothing, but in everything by prayer and supplication, with thanksgiving, let your requests be made known to God; and the peace of God, which surpasses all understanding, will guard your hearts and minds through Christ Jesus. (Philippians 4:6–8)

I'm a Stroke Survivor, *and* I Play One on TV

It was early in 2009 when I got a call from a former art director I'd worked with for many years. She visited me in the hospital and, as I recall, brought me several really dark books to read. She called to ask if I'd be interested in working on a public service announcement TV spot for the Virginia Department of Health on stroke symptom awareness. Thinking I might be the most qualified ad writer in the Commonwealth of Virginia to develop a powerful message on this topic, I immediately agreed to help in any way I could.

I was quite surprised to learn a couple of days later that my art director friend had already hired a copywriter, also a good, longtime friend and an excellent writer to write the script. What they both wanted from me was to play the role of a stroke victim in the commercial. This threw me for a loop on several levels. While I'd written hundreds of commercials and directed a handful, I'd never been in front of the camera before. Was I capable of acting? And was I capable of acting like someone who'd *just* suffered a stroke as the script called for? More importantly, did I want to?

It was a pretty powerful script where the viewer sees blurry scenes and surreal images of wheelchair wheels, IV trees and people in scrubs racing through a busy hospital hallway. Then the voice-over announcer explains the five symptoms of a stroke by asking questions:

- Walk—Is balance off?
- Talk—Is speech slurred or mouth drooping?

- Reach—Is there weakness on one side of the body?
- Sight—Is there loss of vision or partial blindness?
- Feel—Do you have a severe headache?

At this point, the scene cuts to a rather pathetic-looking stroke victim who, in slurred speech, explains, "If you have any of these symptoms, call 911, immediately. Or you could ignore the symptoms … like I did."

I kept weighing the decision. Every time I talked myself out of doing it, I felt guilty, thinking if I could do something (no matter how tiny) to clue even one person as to what the symptoms of a stroke are, wouldn't I be remiss if I didn't do so? The other side of this coin was, do I really want to go back to a hospital (it was to actually be shot in the hospital where I was born in 1956), get in a hospital gown, put on an ID bracelet, sit in a wheelchair and, for a good six hours, relive what I'd worked so hard to put in my past?

Before I had to make my decision, the Virginia Department of Health wanted me to audition. I drove up to Richmond and went to a casting director's office (yet another friend from my past) and read/slurred my lines, acting as if my stroke had happened just a few days prior. Given that the left side of my mouth still droops a bit, I didn't have to act that much. I tucked my left hand into my wrist and, while delivering my lines, looked up and down shyly at the camera as if embarrassed about what I was saying. The folks at the Virginia Department of Health liked what they saw, however—isn't there always a however?

While I am definitely balding, I wear what hair I have fairly long, and I've worn a beard nearly consistently since college. The Department of Health thought losing the beard would make my drooping mouth more evident and a good haircut would make me look like someone who gave a rat's ass about their appearance.

These two requests weren't deal breakers as far as I was concerned, but I still wasn't sure how emotionally comfortable I was about reliving the worst incident in my life. My psychologist should have received hazard pay for having to hear me captain both debate teams, ad nauseam.

It was coming down to the deadline for my decision. My art director and copywriter friends were strongly encouraging me, saying how much I brought to the script in the audition (a trick I use when directing talent and want them to dig a little deeper). I hope it was because of a sincere desire to educate the world, or at least Virginia, about the warning signs of stroke and not some egocentric desire to be liked by my friends that I agreed to do the spot.

The shoot was just a week away. I went ahead and lost the beard a good week in advance in case I caused any major injuries to my face. Then I asked a very stylish friend in Richmond who he had cut his hair and made an appointment with his guy for the day before the shoot. I took it upon myself *not* to shave for two days prior, assuming my character had been in the hospital a day or two and would have something slightly greater than a five o'clock shadow (and if they didn't like it, I could shave on set).

Upon arriving at the hospital, I got very nervous, questioning whether I'd made the right decision. I'm not sure why I recall this so vividly, but this hospital was the last building I've been in that had a bank of payphones. (In fact, one of those phones is probably where my dad called his mother to tell her that her latest grandson had been born.) Once I got upstairs to the actual shoot location, I started having regrets. A flood of sensory flashbacks to three years prior hit me. I'd been instructed to bring a bathrobe to wear during breaks and lunch as my wardrobe was an open-backed hospital gown. They faked an IV going into my arm, and my makeup was *Walking Dead* pale.

Possibly the most unnerving thing to me was having this guy who played a nurse pushing me around in a wheelchair all day. The day in late 2006 when I officially didn't need a wheelchair anymore was such a breakthrough day that getting back in one just felt wrong.

We finished around four o'clock in the afternoon just as sleet started falling outside. Everyone couldn't have been nicer. Two people from the Virginia Department of Health and a very nice woman from the American Heart Association (who later sent me a copy of the AHA Cookbook as a thank-you gift), as well as folks from the ad agency, all complimented me on my acting debut. And swan song.

I left the shoot fairly tired, more emotionally than physically. I had dinner with a couple of friends, returned to my hotel, and drove home the next morning. About a week later I received a call from the head honcho at the ad agency that created the PSA, telling me they were planning an event for March to launch the stroke awareness campaign, which included posters, direct mail, online promotion and the TV spot. The campaign was targeting the rural population in western Virginia, where the highest incidence of stroke-related deaths occurred annually. Therefore, the event/press conference was to be held in Harrisonburg, Virginia, and I was asked to attend. Again, I debated doing this. I hadn't seen the finished commercial and worried that I'd done a crappy job and would be embarrassed.

The person from the agency said it was important to her, and the public relations firm felt it was newsworthy because an actual stroke victim portrayed a stroke victim. Plus Harrisonburg is a pretty little university town in the Virginia mountains where my mother's family held annual reunions. I said yes.

We all met up in Harrisonburg the evening before the event. At dinner, a gentleman from the PR firm, a really nice guy I still stay in touch with, asked if I'd say a few words after they premièred the PSA. In truth, he didn't so much ask me as told me I'd be making a few remarks after they showed the spot. I *hate* public speaking as much as I hate having a catheter inserted—or removed. This added to my nervousness and added another glass of wine to the dinner tab.

Upon returning to my hotel room, I tried writing remarks for my turn at the podium the next morning. Realizing this was just making me more nervous, I decided I'd wing it. I mean, how high could their expectations be when it came to remarks from a guy who'd experienced brain damage?

But I was totally unprepared. Once at the venue, a nice, medium-sized confab room with rows of chairs in a fairly new hospital, my anxiety grew upon seeing the number of chairs. And as people started filling those chairs, it got worse. The event opened with a couple of doctors sharing stats on strokes in Virginia and why the western part of the commonwealth had more than its share of victims (less educated about health issues, people don't regularly see their doctors, hospitals are farther away from homes in rural areas, etc.). This explained the need for the campaign. Next, the gentleman I mentioned from the PR firm got up to share what public relations efforts were being undertaken to better educate the general public about stroke symptoms. Then he introduced my former art director partner, who showed the various advertising pieces of the puzzle—posters, direct mail, Internet web banners, and so forth— and then she cued the audio-visual guy in the back of the room to play the PSA.

Remember, I hadn't seen the finished product, and here it was about to be projected on a larger-than-life screen. It was a sixty-second spot, and it was at about the forty-five-second mark when I would come on screen and start my "If you have any of these symptoms ..." spiel. It was at that point in watching the PSA I thought I was going to come unglued. When I saw my white-as-a-ghost face, I averted my eyes to the floor so I didn't have to see the screen. I tried to imagine a song in my head so I couldn't hear my slurred, "If you have any of these symptoms" call to action.

The spot ended, the lights came back up, people applauded, and I was mortified. But I couldn't stay that way for long because I was introduced to come up and say a few words.

How what happened next happened is beyond me. Where these words came from is a mystery. I'm sure this isn't verbatim, but I think it's pretty close:

> (Applause) Thank you. I'm happy to be here today. After deliberating, I decided to appear in this PSA because I think it's vital everyone knows the symptoms of a stroke. I certainly didn't know them when I had my stroke. Nor did my wife; however, she had enough sense to realize something was terribly wrong. I didn't have the blinding

headache and wasn't aware of the numbness that was quickly taking over the left side of my body. That's why it made total sense to me when I told my wife, "If you love me, you won't call 911." She ignored me. So, like I said, I'm happy to be here today.

My entire speech on the stage was probably shorter than my introduction. I think I was about to say something else, but this little voice in my head told me I'd nailed the dismount, shut up, walk back to your seat and be done. It wasn't a "drop the mic" moment, but the guy from the PR firm mouthed the word *wow* at me. And for the first time since this little stunt started, I felt good.

That was in 2009. I still haven't watched the entire spot all the way through. And I doubt I ever will. However, if you care to see it, go to http://www.youtube.com/watch?v=sa1DcyW4A-Y.

Do We Really Need to Get God Involved in This?

There's a quote from Mother Teresa I've always liked and thought about frequently following the stroke and during my recovery. "I know God will not give me anything I can't handle. I just wish that He didn't trust me so much."

It was shortly after moving to North Carolina and obtaining a note from my new neurologist that my wife and I ventured to the DMV to obtain a pair of handicapped parking permits. I was still in a wheelchair and was parked near the window while Cristie waited in line to fill out the required paperwork. There were empty chairs around me. This blond woman, probably in her twenties, took a seat near my wheelchair, leaned over, and asked, "Why are you in a wheelchair?" Upon telling her I'd had a stroke, she replied, "Why do you think you had a stroke?" I started feeling uncomfortable and thought she was getting too personal, but I answered honestly, saying it was poor lifestyle choices and not taking better care of myself. I barely had this out of my mouth when she said, "So, basically, you had a stroke because you sinned."

Now I was extremely uncomfortable and feeling judged by someone who was around my son's age. When I feel this way, I tend to attempt to joke my way out of the corner. "If smoking, eating an occasional cheeseburger and not exercising enough is your take on sin, I guess I'm guilty," I said.

"Or perhaps you offended God in some other manner," she responded. Now I was getting a bit angry and wishing I'd waited in the car. While I should have kept my mouth shut, I instead argued, "Well, I guess I didn't piss Him off too badly because I lived to tell about it, didn't I?" That was about the moment Cristie, having finished our business, came over and wheeled me back to the car, ending my little theological boxing match.

But my comment about *living to tell about it* stuck with me. Why did I survive? Did God spare me?

In late 2006, I was receiving outpatient physical therapy at a YMCA near our house. My therapist, who is a devout Christian, had me working on a machine in the gym when she was called away for a moment. Instead of having me stop my workout, she asked this large, young, African American gentleman who was a trainer at the Y to spot me. We struck up a conversation, and I learned he was an aspiring pastor.

Skip ahead to the first week in 2007 when, during my PT session, my therapist asked if I remembered the guy who'd spotted me a few weeks earlier. I told her I did and that I had liked the guy. She proceeded to tell me he'd been hired by a church, and she invited me to the service the next Sunday, even providing me with a little crudely drawn map to help me find the place.

My wife, who had found her faith many years earlier but never pushed me too hard to follow her walk, was very pleasantly surprised when she got home from work and I announced, "There's a church I think I'd like to try." Mind you, Cristie's church in Baltimore had been very ethnically diverse, so she was excited further when I explained this was primarily an African American church.

Sunday came, and off we went to church. And I will tell you I have never felt more genuinely welcomed somewhere ever in my entire life. I even got a shout-out from the pulpit when the pastor pointed at me and said, "Oh, look, there's the guy from the weight room at the Y." The message was good and moving, the praise and worship team sang beautifully, and, following the service, more and more people made a point of coming up to Cristie and me to welcome us.

That was nine years ago. We have since become members of the church, and I was baptized. I joined the media ministry, which is just another name for the AV team that runs the sound board, assembles and runs the PowerPoint presentation for the sermon, records the sermon, and burns CDs. Cristie was even ordained a deaconess in 2015.

The News and Observer (Raleigh's daily newspaper) featured a photograph of my baptism to accompany an article about racial integration in modern southern churches. In the article, I'm quoted as saying, "Who knew a middle-aged white couple could bring ethnic diversity to a church in North Carolina."

So, yes, I did find a faith and I have a testimony, and a small part of that touches on my stroke. But my walk with the Lord has nothing to do with me looking to be absolved from some stroke-inducing sin. And while I do pray for health, I don't attend church believing it will spare me from the possibility of a second stroke.

I also feel I am more liberal-minded than most members of our church. And am sure that if my fellow congregants were to read this book, some might have issues with the few swear words I've used to season this epistle.

Recently, while walking into church, an older gentleman walked up alongside me in the parking lot and said, "You don't need that cane. Throw it away, fall to your knees, and ask the good Lord to heal you." While I respect this gentleman's sincerely deep faith, I'm pretty skeptical about parking-lot miracles, and miracles in general. And in Andy's real post-stroke world, if I were to throw away my cane, the chances of me falling to my knees would grow exponentially.

Come On, I've Already Done the Hospital

As mentioned previously, while in rehab following the stroke, I was diagnosed with a condition that caused the head of my left femur (the ball in the ball and socket of my left hip) to collapse and break apart. This condition is called avascular necrosis, or AVN for short. Not knowing how to spell *avascular necrosis*, I first Googled "AVN" and landed on the page for Adult Video News. These are the folks who give out the porn industry's equivalent of Oscars.

I've known since the day of the diagnosis that a hip replacement was in my future, but I kept putting it off despite the fact that it was growing more painful and doing little to secure my balance. However, I diligently went to see an orthopaedic surgeon annually for an assessment and every year talked myself into putting it off, not that my doctor at the time was shooting emergency flares in the sky indicating it was a serious issue. My mind-set was, "I don't really need to do hospital again." Then, in early 2014, I found a joint-replacement surgeon who made me feel confident about going ahead with the operation. I timed the whole thing out so my advertising clients had all the work they needed from me through mid-June and I'd be fully recovered in time for Cristie's and my twenty-fifth anniversary trip in September. To use a phrase that causes my psychologist to shake her head disapprovingly, I pulled the trigger.

My hip replacement was elective surgery, and, going in, I knew I was going to be in the hospital for a few nights, as well as a couple of days for physical and occupational therapy. Two weeks prior to the surgery, my doctor sent me to the hospital for pre-op stuff—filling out forms, giving blood, talking to the anesthesiologist—and something called "hip class." Hip class was basically a *valuable* two-hour session of FAQs hosted by a surgical nurse, social worker and physical therapist where "What can I expect?" was explained thoroughly. I applaud my doctor's practice for making such a resource available and appreciated the opportunity, especially the chance to speak with the therapist about how physical therapy would proceed given that I already had a deficit on the left side of my body from the stroke, as well as the left patella. I was told I wasn't the first to present this issue but definitely among the youngest. I was reassured and ready to proceed.

The day of the surgery was May 6, and I repeatedly joked that I hoped no one on my surgical team had attended a Cinco de Mayo celebration the night before. I made it clear if I entered the operating room and there was a busted piñata and empty tequila bottles littering the floor, I was out of there immediately! That wasn't to be the case. Instead, I sat in the general waiting area of the hospital's surgery center with my wife and our pastor until my name was called to go to pre-op. Walking back to that area, I became acutely aware that I was walking with a cane but wouldn't be doing so for the next few weeks (little did I know just how many weeks). I believe I relinquished my cane to Cristie once I was shown a seat on a gurney and told to change into the provided hospital gown.

I was quite nervous about this whole ordeal and had expressed this to basically anyone who'd listen. It was my surgeon who first said, "I understand. I thoroughly understand," when I expressed that I didn't fear dying in the operating room, yet I was terrified of forming a thromboembolus (or, to use layman's terms, "throwing a clot"), causing another stroke either on the operating table or a couple of weeks thereafter and *living*. The thought of starting over from scratch on stroke recovery terrified me, and I'd rather sit it out in the mortuary.

I brought this fear with me into pre-op, but some really, really nice person took it from me. He put it in a bag with my other personal possessions upon giving me an epidural while I sat on the edge of the gurney, followed by an injection of some magical elixir into my IV tube.

The next thing I recall is startling awake. For some reason, I had anticipated gently floating out of the anesthetic/post-surgical fog, yet instead I crash-landed rather suddenly. And while I don't remember anyone shaking me or assiduously trying to return me to the here and now, I do remember anyone and everyone who walked past the foot of my bed (was I now indeed in a hospital bed?) encouraging me to pump my feet and wiggle my toes. And for the next ninety minutes or so, I'd consistently disappoint these slightly blurry-looking people donning a rainbow of different-colored scrubs as my toes and ankles refused to play their reindeer games.

Eventually, however, I was deemed hospital room–worthy. And almost immediately, I flashed back to my room on the fourth floor at Henrico Doctors' Hospital (HDH) in February 2006. For a moment, I thought someone was screwing with me by attempting to make my room look like the HDH twin. The layout was identical from my bed to the door to the hallway and bathroom to my left, the window to the right, and a wall clock directly in front of me. The clock haunted me a little. In Baltimore, I worked with an amazingly talented art director who grew as close to me as a brother. The more time I spent with Jim, the more I inherited some of his traits. For example, pictures of any type hung crookedly on the wall bothered him tremendously—to the extent that we nearly got kicked out of a restaurant in London after Jim insisted on leveling the establishment's entire collection of wall-pretties—and I grew to share this little idiosyncrasy.

It was a result of this quirk that my eye was continually drawn to the clock in my room and the fact the twelve and the six weren't aligned. All of the other numbers on the face seemed to line up okay. It could have been an optical illusion given that the *Staples* logo, which is a bit cockeyed to begin with, was between the ten and the two but favored the ten side. I seriously doubt that the fact I was on a large dose of a powerful opioid analgesics played any role here.

So why was I so preoccupied with the clock? Well, remember when I suggested that you never check in to a hospital that doesn't offer *The Travel Channel*? Now you can add Discovery Communication's similar offering in the world of must-have cable channels to that list with *Destination America*. This hospital's television lineup offered neither (I should have asked at hip class). Instead, entertainment became the cavalcade of visitors and medical professionals who paraded through my room, and I quickly learned their appointed (according to that clock) rounds.

Initially, vitals were taken every couple of hours. A nurse would arrive with her or his portable blood pressure machine on a stick with wheels and a small basket to carry the blood oxygen meter, electronic thermometer and little box of plastic thermometer sheaths (or thermo-condoms, as I like to call them). These stat takers were remarkably efficient, wheeling in, Velcroing a cuff to my upper arm, clipping a finger, sticking a probe under the tongue, recording my digits and then gone in a flash. Efficient and impressive.

Then there was the 4:00 a.m. visit from the phlebotomist—a word I love for the sole reason that the average person could guess ten thousand times what it means and never get it right. That is because the average person is not a Greek philologist who understands the literal root of the word interprets to "one who makes an incision into blood vessels." So, yes, at four o'clock every morning, a young woman or man would enter my room, tie off my upper arm with an elastic band, slap the inside fold of my elbow a few times, draw a couple of test tubes full of blood and then leave. Good day to you, young phlebotomist.

By six o'clock, my blood had been through a battery of tests, and my surgeon's physician's assistant had received an analysis on, well, me. I know this because that's what time the PA would show up with my file and report, "Your X, Y and Z look good. Your M is a little high, but that's to be expected this soon after surgery, but overall, everything's fine. The doctor will be by in a while. I'll see you tomorrow." Or something to that effect. In addition, she'd peek at the incision on my left hip and then move on to her next charge.

Finally, the surgeon himself would appear, normally around seven or seven thirty. He, too, would examine the incision, compliment himself on a job well done and reassure me that I'd be as good as new by mid to late June. In fact, on more than one occasion, I recall him saying, "By the first of July, you're going to be so glad you did this."

The evening following the surgery, a physical therapist came to my room to help me get out of bed, stand for a moment, and then get back in bed. I barely recall this. I do, however, remember being introduced to the big blue wedge of discomfort. Basically there are three things one is forbidden to do following total hip replacement: (1) bend past ninety degrees at the waist, (2) twist in either direction at the waist, and (3) cross one's legs. No crossing is allowed whatsoever, even at the ankles. Hence the blue foam rubber wedge strategically placed between my legs and Velcroed to said legs while in bed, especially while sleeping. It wasn't some desire I had to cross my legs that made this thing uncomfortable. It was uncomfortable because flippin' foam rubber doesn't breathe, and under a sheet in a warm hospital room, it not only doesn't breathe—it suffocates.

The day after surgery, I started physical therapy with a gentleman who seemed desperate to become the spokesperson for tough love. Not only did he push me in my therapy, which I understand and appreciate, but he also repeatedly told me I needed a haircut and should shave my beard as a gray beard made me look old. It was an adding-insult-(literally)-to-injury kind of therapy. I was quite glad when he didn't show up the next day and was replaced by a pleasant woman who genuinely asked Cristie and me what she could do to help us face the challenges waiting at home. This included the number of steps to get in our back door, the height of the bed, and needed equipment like a raised toilet seat, walker, and so on. I was allowed and encouraged to bear full weight on both legs. The therapist taught me how to climb the three steps to our back porch using the walker and walking backward. I've tried a couple of times here to explain this technique in words, but I'd need to show you for you to totally get it. We were assured that someone from the hospital's in-home health services would be in touch with us nearly immediately upon getting home.

Going home—let's discuss this for a moment. There was a lot of discussion about whether or not Cristie would be able to care for me once I got home. And what if I fell while transferring from the wheelchair to the bed or toilet or vice versa? For a while there was talk of my going to a rehab facility for a spell. This was all very reminiscent of leaving the hospital post-stroke. This time, however, Cristie said she thought she could handle my being home if she had some backup help. Introducing Kristine.

Kristine worked at the seminary where Cristie is employed. She is a young, sweet, former Miss Georgia contestant whom we sort of mutually adopted three years prior to all of this. Usually, we'd have a movie and dinner night once a week and Academy Awards parties and Halloween celebrations together. But Kristine kind of moved in (stayed overnight) once I returned home in the event Cristie needed help. Everyone felt a little better knowing that this able-bodied thirty-year-old was close at hand in the event things went south.

I was discharged from the hospital on the Friday following the surgery. And when Cristie called the in-home health people the following Monday, they fell all over themselves apologizing for not getting in touch sooner (like over the weekend) and seemed quite concerned that we were going to rat them out to my orthopaedist. They scheduled a physical therapy and occupational therapy evaluation, as well as a visiting nurse checkup within twenty-four hours. All three of these individuals were great, especially Jim, the OT, who had been my in-home therapist following the knee surgery in 2007.

Everything was fine until the following Thursday. A different physical therapist was sent to the house, and her agenda for that session was to teach me how to side-step up and down stairs. For the previous nine days since the surgery, I'd worn a sneaker on my right foot and a non-skid hospital sock on the left (Google it if you don't know what I mean). This therapist (let's call her Eris, after the Greek goddess of chaos, strife and discord) put a sock and the other sneaker on my still-swollen left foot, and, using the walker, outside Eris and I went to the side porch where there are three narrow brick steps with a wrought-iron railing. At the time

I thought, *I haven't worn a shoe on this foot since the surgery. Shouldn't I try out this new hip-and-shoe combo on a level surface once or twice before attempting to climb stairs?* Thought it; didn't say it out loud.

We started at the top, and I successfully managed to climb down from the top step to the bottom. In retrospect, I think gravity may have helped me here, because going back up was a lot more difficult. I put my right foot on the bottom step, trying to allow enough room for my left foot to follow suit. While I was bearing weight on my left leg, my arms were giving the railing the majority of my body weight. The therapist took note of this as my left foot settled on the first step. Eris said, "Let's try the next step, but this time put more weight on your left leg." My right foot went up and settled on the second step as I shifted the predominance of my weight onto my left leg. That's when I both heard and felt the snap in my hip. Let me be honest here—I may have imagined hearing a snap.

The miracle here is that I didn't swear. The second miracle—I didn't fall. I hung onto that railing as if my life depended on it, and, for all I knew, it did. In addition, I bellowed, something I don't recall having ever done before. The physical therapist remained calm, telling me to just step up to the next step while telling Cristie to grab a chair and put it on the porch next to the top step. Doing as I was told, I took the next step, and the pain doubled and I started feeling nauseated. Now all I could think about was planting my ass in the chair. Cristie was already (or so it seemed) on the phone to my surgeon's office. I finally sat, thinking that was going to relieve the pain. That wasn't the first miscalculation I'd made that day.

Meanwhile, my doctor's office instructed Cristie to get me back to the hospital. The therapist repeatedly told me that I'd popped the new hip out of the socket and that it could easily be popped back in at the hospital. No big deal. It was at that moment when my claim that there's no greater pain than a kidney stone was permanently put to rest. Nothing was easing the hurt, but just hearing the ambulance's siren even in the distance meant I was one second closer to a hypodermic needle full of something delicious.

The ride to the hospital was excruciating as even the slightest bump or turn caused tremendous pain. I do need to give a shout-out here to the kind, young, female EMT who sat in the back of the ambulance taking my blood pressure, which was orbiting near the International Space Station, every two minutes or so and trying to engage me in conversation to keep my mind off the pain. It was a valiant, yet futile, effort. I swore at the time I'd remember this woman's name, but alas, I don't. So sorry.

About forty-five minutes later, we pulled into the emergency room entrance, where I was whisked to a little curtained cubicle. Cristie and Kristine soon joined me. Fortunately, the file on my recent hospital stay was available to the ER staff, so I was asked relatively few questions. The doctor tending to my care echoed the therapist's prophecy of "hip popped out of socket." He said they'd take me to another room, dope me up, and pop it back in. No biggie. But first, let's just get an x-ray to make sure.

Following the x-ray, this young doc returned to my cubicle with a look on his face like he'd just been dumped by his girlfriend via text. Falling all over himself apologizing, he explained that the new hip was still very much in its socket. However, my femur was broken, and I'd need a second surgery. I recall wanting to cry, but I stopped myself when I saw how upset Cristie and Kristine were. It was about then that a nurse delivered my dinner, which I hadn't ordered. And while I had zero appetite, I do recall that the poached salmon looked pretty good and nothing like you'd expect to come out of a hospital kitchen.

So, for a spring when you couldn't go more than twenty minutes without hearing Pharrell Williams' "Happy," I sure wasn't feeling it.

Back to Six-West and a different room with the exact same layout. Surgery was scheduled for the next day, and I recall very little from the time I was wheeled into my new room to waking up in recovery following surgery. I'm certain they had me doped to the gills given the pain I was in. And what exactly was this surgery I was about to undergo? All I knew was my femur was busted and needed to be "set." Other than that, I was clueless and totally trusting my surgeon and my wife.

From what I was told, my first surgery (actual time in the OR) was a little over an hour and resulted in fourteen staples. So much for wearing a thong at the beach that summer. Surgery number two lasted nearly four hours, and I had forty staples to show for it. Now even wearing a Speedo was out.

Once I did come to in recovery, I got to play the "try to pump your feet" game again. This time, however, instead of being encouraged by medical personnel passing the foot of my bed, I had my very own nurse seated beside my bed monitoring my blood pressure, oxygen level, and other vitals. What I took from this was that procedure two was a bit more serious than procedure one. Once I was finally okayed to leave recovery and return to my room, I slightly panicked as I recalled that a physical therapist had me standing about four hours after returning to my room following the first procedure. This time, I hurt badly, and the notion of having to stand seemed impossible and torturous. Fortunately, my instructions were to heal with the only exercises being to pump my feet frequently and squeeze my glutes (butt cheeks) a few times hourly. Then someone, probably a therapist, brought me another big blue wedge of discomfort.

I think it was the next day that Cristie came into my room with a lidded white plastic container that was about the size of a tub you'd be carrying if someone asked you to bring the potato salad or coleslaw to a neighborhood block party. She opened it and reached in (à la the same way a magician reaches inside his top hat to pull out a rabbit) and pulled out something I didn't immediately recognize. It was then Cristie explained that it was my original replacement hip and how, following procedure number two, my surgeon presented her with this piece of titanium topped with a pinkish ceramic ball, explaining they had to take this one out to put in the second prosthetic hip with a longer femoral stem. They then wrapped the busted femur with wire. He went on to explain that we'd already purchased the first replacement hip for the whopping sum of $20,000, and thus we should have it as a souvenir. I think this was the good doctor's bad attempt at humor. So now we're the proud owners of a twenty-grand paperweight in a potato salad container. Upon further deliberation, I also concluded the replacement hip could be converted into a door knocker or marital aid.

Despite having a souvenir of a hip replacement gone awry, I was still curious as to what had happened. Please recall that at no point in this entire tale was I more sedated than at this time, meaning the accuracy of my memory here is fairly questionable, but Cristie says I'm definitely in the ballpark. Upon asking the physician assistant if fracturing the femur during total hip replacement was common, she said it happens and is a "tolerated" risk. This seemed a bit cavalier to me. But she went on to explain that when the replacement hip's femoral stem is hammered (yes, literally hammered) into the thighbone, there's the risk of the stem kind of acting like a splitting wedge on a log. This pioneer-like analogy made me both nod in understanding and wince in recalling the femur breaking. Basically, the femur fractured during the initial surgery, but my surgeon couldn't see it and it didn't stand out in the post-surgery x-ray. And when in therapy I put all my weight on my left leg by stepping up to the next brick step with my right, the fracture became a true break.

Now there was very little I could do in terms of therapy because, until the break healed, bearing weight on my left leg was not an option. And neither was just lying around in the hospital. I was rehab facility bound. The question was where my insurance company wanted me to go and where there was a room for me. As it turned out, the hospital I was in owns two rehab facilities—one adjacent to the hospital and another fourteen miles away. The latter is thirty-three miles away from our home in Wake Forest, which is inconvenient for Cristie, and connected to a rest home. Guess who had a bed with my name on it?

Rest home!? For Christ's sake. A rest home is where your grandmother's friends who smelled funny went to die after breaking their hips. And didn't I just basically break my hip or do something somewhat similar?

The day to transfer to the rehab/rest home came, and I basically waited around all day for the ambulance crew to show up to transport me. By around four o'clock that afternoon, I assumed I'd spend another night in the hospital when, lo and behold, Frick and Frack from Keystone Cops Ambulance Service showed up to take me for a ride. I'm making fun of this situation because these two medical transport professionals argued the entire fourteen-mile trip about how to get to the facility. Mind you, this was after each of them had told me what a nice facility it is, meaning this wasn't their first trip there. While this trip wasn't nearly as painful as my ambulance ride to the hospital, it was still kind of uncomfortable as these two bozos bickered and made phone calls to get directions. Hell, I had my iPhone on me and could have gotten us there, but I was pretty doped up and didn't feel like getting into the fray. Plus, I was out of the hospital and actually in a moving vehicle. This was as close to an adventure as I was going to have for a while.

Upon arriving at the facility, reality came crashing down as my gurney was maneuvered through the halls past elderly people in parked wheelchairs and opened doors, revealing primarily bedridden women watching either *Maury* or *Judge Judy*. In defense of Judith Sheindlin, my mother, who could be pretty anti-Semitic at times, was a huge fan, and I have watched a couple of episodes for lack of other entertainment sources. That said, I had barely arrived in my semiprivate room when I was told, for the first of what would become dozens of pronouncements, that I was the youngest patient in the population. Quickly, back to the term *semiprivate*, which yourdictionary.com defines (quoting *Webster's New World College Dictionary*, 2010, Wiley Publishing) as "partly but not completely private; specif., designating or of a hospital room with two, three, or sometimes four beds." In my case, fortunately, *semiprivate* meant merely two beds. This room didn't look anything like my room at Henrico Doctors' or the room I'd just left, the most obvious difference being the inclusion of a second bed.

Unfortunately, the other bed in my room was inhabited by a gentleman who slept most of the day so he could turn on his TV at eleven o'clock at night and turn up the volume one click every thirty minutes until six o'clock in the morning or whenever his wife arrived (I'm assuming and being sarcastic here, okay?). When my roommate's friends, wife, or other relatives would visit, they'd hold conversations and turn the room into what I can only imagine would be Hades for English majors. I didn't even know there was such a thing as a quadruple negative until I heard it with my own ears. A quadruple negative, by the way, is a double positive.

Now if the TV hadn't been enough to prevent me from sleeping, add in my third big blue wedge of discomfort, general pain from the incision, and swelling so severe in my left leg and ankle that I thought my skin was ripping at times. Pain meds and sleep aids did little to help. By day three, at dear Kristine's suggestion, I looked up white noise machine apps on my phone and found something called Sleep Pillow Sounds, which features a good seventy sound effects. That night, I selected something akin to the sound of a train off in the distance with a gentle rain. And while it helped, the earbuds would cause me to wake up if I flattened either side of my head on the pillow. Fortunately, I was moved to a private room the next day. (Cristie had been working on this behind the scenes, God bless her.)

The new room did look a bit more like the hospital rooms from my past, except the wall clock glowed with an eerie green hue circling its face when the room was dark. This came in handy when I didn't want to turn on a light to see just how long I'd been lying awake in bed. Even though the room was quiet, my body continued to complain quite loudly.

I have to give the staff at this facility pretty high marks, with the exception of one young nurse who attempted to strap me into the blue wedge of discomfort while it was inverted, meaning she tried to cram the wide base of the triangle into my groin region and the narrow point of the wedge at my feet. When I asked her to retrieve another nurse, it was obvious I'd hurt her feelings. But I was nothing but genuinely grateful to her and every one of the other nurses who brought me ice packs for my hip and my "I swear the skin is ripping apart" ankle. I seriously put the facility's ice maker through its paces. One of my occupational therapists is fond of saying, "Ice takes the flame out of inflammation."

I'm certain one of the reasons I got such good care from the staff was that one of my clients sent me a rather large gift basket filled with a variety of chocolate treats consisting of cookies, Hershey's Kisses, truffles and Godiva chocolates. Whenever a nurse would deliver an ice pack or pain pills or help me transfer from the bed to the wheelchair or back, I'd tell them to help themselves to something from the basket. It was funny, as some people were shy and would only take one piece, while others made the most of the situation and would take a couple of snacks for then and put one or two more in the pocket of their scrubs for later. One nurse I was quite fond of was allergic to chocolate, so I had Cristie bring her a couple of cookies from my favorite Wake Forest bakery.

Therapy at this facility included PT and OT. OT was primarily focused on personal hygiene (bathing, using the toilet, and so forth), while PT focused on upper body strength and pivoting on my right foot without bearing any weight on my left. This eventually proved quite useful as I became more dependent on using a walker and had to use the railings on handicap adapted toilets. The facility had a very nice little, well-manicured outdoor area off the wing I was in, and I spent as much time out there as I could. The one real blessing of this whole ordeal is that it was a remarkably pleasant spring and summer, far cooler and less humid than previous years I'd encountered in North Carolina.

If you'd asked me how long I was in the rehab facility/nursing home, prior to asking Cristie to look up the actual dates reported in our insurance explanation of benefits, I would have sworn I was there for five weeks. In reality, I was there about half that long.

Getting home was a bit of a challenge unto itself. I couldn't climb into or out of a car, so we had to hire a wheelchair transport service to cart me from the facility to home. The guy who showed up with the van reeked of cigarettes and had the personality of a cinderblock. He didn't speak once the entire thirty-three miles, nor did he bother with his turn signal when changing lanes, which was frequently—which may explain that while Cristie left the facility at the same time I did, we beat her home. There I discovered friends had reinstalled the ramp we'd had built when I busted my patella in 2007 so that I could get in the back door. Unfortunately, I didn't have house keys, and Mr. Personality didn't have any inclination to let me sit in his air-conditioned van until Cristie got home. It was a drop and run. So there I sat in my wheelchair on a hot tarmac driveway with my plastic urinal in a plastic shopping bag and my cell phone. Fortunately, Cristie arrived five minutes later, quite unhappy.

What did make us both very happy was that home health services kicked in almost immediately. I loved both my in-home OT and PT, who seemed to care about my state of mind as much as my physical well-being. The hospital initially wanted to send Eris back as my physical therapist. And while I'm certain she's great at her job, either out of superstition or just generally not wishing to be reminded of any aspect of the femur breaking, I requested a different therapist. Fortunately, they were able to accommodate.

But I didn't have therapy every day, and Cristie needed to make an appearance at work every now and then. The seminary was very gracious and understanding. They provided her with a laptop that I jokingly suggested had been manufactured in the 1920s. It wasn't particularly reliable and couldn't hold a wi-fi connection for more than five minutes at a time, thus tempting a woman who works for a seminary to go off on very un-Christian-like rants. So periodically, she needed to go to her actual office to get actual work accomplished. However, I really couldn't be left alone. I was in a wheelchair and needed assistance with bathing, using the toilet, fixing something to eat, and other everyday tasks. Cristie found an outfit called Home Instead Senior Care. Essentially, it's a franchise operation that provides screened, trained, reliable and professional caregivers who come to your home to look after folks, well, like me. I balked at this at first, primarily because I was put off by the words *senior care*. While these women were kind and polite, they still felt like babysitters to me. One woman would talk about how the pastor at her church would call out people in her congregation who weren't tithing enough and how she was worried she would be next. Another woman enjoyed cooking, so we'd fix dinner together, usually a slow-cooker recipe. But most days, I'd wheel myself to my office and work while the caregiver stayed in the kitchen reading, knitting or working on puzzles. And more often than not, I'd let the person leave before her shift was scheduled to be over. A similar company to Home Instead is called Visiting Angels. I'm glad we didn't go with them because what if they had screwed up and accidentally sent the Angel of Death?

Thinking back on the whole hip/femur debacle, it was far harder emotionally, physically, and psychologically than the stroke. And I can blame that on a number of reasons.

- I was in a nursing home where I occasionally saw patients just parked in their wheelchairs in hallways for hours. Was I looking at my future?
- The therapies weren't helping me "get back on my feet" as they had in rehab post-stroke.
- This was not what was supposed to have happened. (Elective surgery, remember? I wouldn't have elected for this.)
- Finally, and probably most importantly, I was in pain like I'd never felt before. While many stroke victims experience a blinding headache at the onset of the stroke, I didn't. In fact, the only time I hurt with the stroke was the night I got my foot caught in the railing of my hospital bed and the few subsequent falls I've experienced. And yes, while coming back from the stroke (relearning everyday things) was terribly frustrating, there was virtually zero physical pain. As I write this, it has been fourteen months since procedure number one and, truth be told, I still hurt—not nearly as badly, but hurt all the same.

And as that pain began to wane and use of my left leg slowly returned, it dawned on me that I was still a stroke survivor with the same physical deficits and issues I had before this hip ordeal, or what became known as the Femur Fiasco of '14. In fact, I am slightly worse for the wear. It seems the spasticity and hypertonicity in my left arm and hand were greater than they had been prior to my first procedure. The reason for this is complicated, but it makes sense. Using my left arm and hand post-stroke required a certain amount of concentration and focus. Prior to the hip debacle, focusing and concentrating on using my arm and, primarily, my hand had become fairly routine. But after procedures one and two, I had to learn how to walk all over again, thus throwing the majority of my mental focus on my left leg and foot rather than allowing an equal balance of concentration on both of my left-side extremities. The trick now was regaining that balance of concentration. So, in physical therapy,

I not only had to learn how to walk *yet* again but also had to go back into OT to regain partial use of my upper left extremity, which I had worked so hard to obtain through many rounds of therapy over the previous seven years. Was I pissed? Was I bitter?

Yes. Yes, I was. Did it get me anywhere? No, not really. The mantra under my breath was, as always, "Adapt, adapt."

I had a dear friend who was an audio engineer and who has since passed on. He had many sayings (some rather wise) that have stuck with me over the years. But one thing he used to say was an acronym that works for me sometimes when things get trying: FIDO.

In other words, "Fuck it. Drive on."

MD Doesn't Stand for *Medical Deity*

Given my many years in the advertising and marketing field, I frequently enjoy looking at vintage ads, commercials, and print ads created before the Federal Trade Commission and other governmental agencies placed restrictions on what could and couldn't be said or claimed. For example, I found a color magazine ad from the 1950s featuring an illustration of a friendly faced, gray-haired gentleman in a shirt and tie. Next to this man is a copy block that reads, "He's one of the busiest men in town. While his door may say *Office Hours 2 to 4*, he's actually on call 24 hours a day. The doctor is a scientist, a diplomat, and a friendly sympathetic human being all in one, no matter how long and hard his schedule." Below this illustration and copy block is the ad's headline: "*According to a recent Nationwide survey:* More Doctors Smoke Camels Than Any Other Cigarette." Similarly, I found an ad for Lucky Strike featuring the headline, "20,679 Physicians say, "Lucky's are *less irritating*."

If you're younger than, let's say, forty, you might find it hard to believe cigarettes were once actually marketed with the endorsement of medical professionals. While the link between cigarettes and health issues had yet to make newspaper headlines in the 1950s, surely some doctors back then had to have acknowledged a link between smoking and emphysema.

But more obvious than that is how tobacco companies realized the power of physicians. *Reader's Digest* polled over one thousand American adults, asking them to rank people of their trustworthiness. Of the fifteen professions tested, doctors came out on top, beating out clergy, educators and philanthropists. Which would explain Big Tobacco's marketing strategy of "Yeah, sure you've got a horrible, phlegm-producing cough and wheeze after climbing one flight of stairs but, hey, doctors say it's okay to smoke."

Whenever a doctor told my mother something she didn't want to hear, she'd say (not to the doctor's face, mind you), "Well, *somebody* had to graduate at the bottom of their class." My point is that we place physicians on ridiculously high pedestals and assume they can do no wrong. That's just not so.

Many years ago, I took my son to an ophthalmologist who specialized in treating children with special needs. We'd been to see this guy a couple of times before, and each time we spent at least two hours in the waiting room. On this particular day, Graham was sitting in my lap, and the doctor was being a tad aggressive while trying to hold my son's eye open. As a consequence, Graham reflexively batted the doctor's arm away, to which the doctor replied, "Would you look at that. Even a vegetable can manage to put up resistance." At that moment, I stood up, carried Graham to his wheelchair, and told his caregiver to take him to the car and I'd be there shortly. As she and Graham left the doctor's office, I turned toward the doctor, who said, "You've got to be kidding me. What's your problem?"

I pointed out that my son has cerebral palsy and is not in a vegetative state, and how dare he say something like that. His response was, "Who's the doctor here, jerk?" This is the only time in my adult life I've ever come close to actually hitting someone. I stormed out of the exam room, walked past the checkout desk without paying, went to the parking lot and hugged my son for a good five minutes. The doctor's practice and I argued for several months about an unpaid bill, but eventually they stopped hounding me when the doctor retired about a year later.

On the other hand, I can't praise my son's pediatric neurologist highly enough. Even after Graham's mother and I divorced, this doctor let me know he was available should I have any questions or concerns about Graham's care, health and well-being. It was Graham's pediatrician who turned us on to this wonderful gentleman.

But in many situations, and in nearly all emergency situations, you don't get to choose your physician. When I busted up my ankle, Cristie drove me to one hospital, but they sent us to a different one because they didn't have an ankle specialist on call that evening. Following x-rays at the second hospital, they called in their sports medicine ortho surgeon who was anything but happy to be there on a Friday night, and he made that abundantly clear. He did my surgery at midnight. I stayed in the hospital overnight, and after learning how to manage going up and down one flight of stairs with a cast on my right foot up to midcalf, I was sent home with instructions to see my surgeon two weeks later.

Here's where it got interesting. Cristie went with me to this first appointment (and every one after that given I couldn't drive with my right foot in a cast) at the doctor's office that he shared with a number of other orthopaedic specialists. Upon entering the examination room, he shook my hand yet completely ignored Cristie. He was pleased with his handiwork, got up and exited the room. Cristie and I sat there for a few minutes waiting for him to return. I mean, he didn't say, "Come back in two weeks," "Don't get the cast wet," "Have a nice day" or "Canadians are extremely polite people." Nothing. Finally, Cristie went out in the hall, found a nurse and asked if Dr. Houdini was planning on coming back. She said no and to just check out at the front desk where they'd schedule my next appointment.

Two weeks later, we were back in the exact same exam room. I know this because of the sports memorabilia that adorned the room. The doc came in, again ignored my wife, and sent me to another room to have my cast removed, staples removed, and a smaller cast put on. I asked the cast-master if I needed to see the doc again before I left. He checked with *somebody* in the hallway and told me they would schedule my next appointment when I checked out.

On the way home, Cristie and I compared notes on these two visits. We both came to the conclusion that this surgeon's practice only allocated a certain amount of time per patient. So prior to going to the next appointment, we composed a list of our questions.

At appointment three, the doctor entered the exam room, and I checked my watch. Again, he didn't acknowledge Cristie. He said my cast would be removed and I was to start physical therapy, and then he headed for the door. Pulling out my list of questions, I asked him to wait because I had a couple of questions. He looked agitated, and then he grabbed my list and went through each, machine-gunning the answers. Then—poof—he vanished. I glanced at my watch. He had spent a total of seven minutes with us.

I know it would be nice to have the old-school doctors' office, à la the Norman Rockwell *Saturday Evening Post* cover. But in truth, today's medical practices are businesses, and all businesses need to run efficiently to be profitable. Basically, this makes us medical consumers rather than patients, which means we have the right to treat those who treat us in the same manner as we would lawyers, CPAs, landscapers, picture framers, booksellers and any other service provider. Of course, this knocks physicians off the ridiculously high pedestal I mentioned earlier. And I'm certainly not implying any disrespect to those in the medical field. I'm just saying that, like with any service provider, make sure you get what you're paying for.

Just like with my busted ankle, neither Cristie nor I had any say as to which (not witch) doctor would be waiting for me when the EMTs delivered me to Henrico Doctors' Hospital on the day of the stroke. This time, however, I hit the jackpot. My neurologist, an African American gentleman who dressed to the nines and wore subtle, pleasant cologne, was caring, reassuring, respectful and patient. He let Cristie ask the same questions dozens of times. Often he'd answer questions we weren't smart enough to know to ask. I recall him coming to my room nearly every night, when he'd pull back the bottom of my sheet, pinch my big toe, and ask, "Do you feel that?" If I said no, which I did most nights, he'd reply, "Well, let's just hope for tomorrow." If he saw me doing therapy, he'd always give me a thumbs-up. He was just a great man and doctor.

As far as the orthopaedic surgeon who replaced my hip is concerned, I was actually seeing a different surgeon for several years prior to going with the doctor I chose. I first saw the original doctor in 2007. Prior to meeting this guy, I was told by several people including therapists, that he was a good doctor but had a lousy bedside manner and could be rude. Initially, I found him to be just the opposite. He took x-rays and said a hip replacement was inevitable, but he wanted to put it off for as long as possible. He also put me on Fosamax, which is normally prescribed for osteoporosis, to help strengthen the bone around my hip socket.

After repeating his "let's push this for as long as possible" stance for several years, he started insisting that we hurry up and do the procedure upon his switching to a different practice. The last time I saw him, I brought along a list of questions, and after answering three of them, he said he didn't have time for any more questions. These two things caused me concern and inspired me to get both a second opinion and a new orthopaedic surgeon. At the suggestion of a therapist friend, I went to see a doctor about forty-five miles east of Wake Forest. He was young; practicing some new, less-invasive hip replacement procedures; and thought I should have my hip replaced, but he wasn't rushing me into it. A few months later, his practice moved even further east to be closer to his preferred hospital. This would have made follow-up visits post-surgery very inconvenient, not to mention a long haul for Cristie to come see me in the hospital every day.

So we asked around, and one name kept coming up in the Raleigh area. And this is how we came to meet my surgeon, whom one of my other doctors refers to as "He Who Thinks He Is God." While I didn't get a true glimpse of the ego my doctor was alluding to, I did see a man who delegated a lot to others on his staff and was quick to tell me what a great job he did—this despite the fact he fractured my femur. (Please see the chapter, "Come On, I've Already Done the Hospital.")

My favorite medical doctor in my corral of physicians is probably my internist. He's funny, personable, a good listener and even better at explaining things. Instead of shaking hands, he fist-bumps during the cold and flu season. Best of all, he ends every appointment with, "If you have any questions, don't hesitate to call me."

I know you didn't ask for it, but here's *my* medical advice.

- Always write down any and all questions you might have and bring that list to your appointment.
- At the very start of your visit, let the doctor, PA, nurse practitioner, or whoever you're seeing know you have some questions, and don't leave until every one of your questions is answered.
- If possible, bring a loved one, family member, or good friend with you to the appointment. Two sets of ears hear better than one.
- Remember, you're a medical consumer. Make sure you get what you're paying for.
- Never be afraid to get a second opinion. Someone once told me she didn't want to get a second opinion because she was afraid if her doctor found out, it might hurt his feelings. I told her if she truly believed that, I might not be able to be her friend.

Hope and Cope

As I write this, I'm at sea with my beloved bride on a cruise. This is our first trip since the hip fiasco, and since seriously applying polish to this book I feel hypersensitive of my condition. I had to show a card that my hip-replacement-ortho doc gave me to get through TSA at the airport, which entitled me to an actual hands-on pat down. It wasn't nearly as exciting as I'd hoped, probably because it was administered by a semi-postpubescent redhead named Carl (according to his nametag) who repeatedly patted my right arm from elbow to wrist. Why? I'm not certain.

Walking up the gangplank onto the ship at a forty-five-degree angle lugging my carry-on proved more tiring, trying and treacherous than I had anticipated. Mind you, the airline had lost our luggage at JFK, and we got in a good ninety minutes late (arriving at the ship around twelve thirty in the morning), so we were a bit on edge about everything.

But now I'm on board, at sea, and relaxed, and I'm taking some time to figure out how to end this missive. The thing that most people who have watched me go through my recovery over the last ten years comment on is how far I've come back. And while in reality it has been a lot of work, it has never felt like a lot of work. It just felt like something that needed to get done. And I've had a remarkable support system.

Prior to moving to Wake Forest, my sister managed to hunt down a physician for me in every medical discipline I required. Anyone who knew my sister would tell you she could get anything accomplished simply because she knew who to talk to. If she didn't know the right person herself, she certainly knew the right person who knew the right person. Upon her death in November 2006, I could have probably sold her Rolodex online for a small fortune. She was just that well connected. Armed with names and phone numbers that my sister provided, Cristie miraculously scored appointments with every one of these doctors for the first week I was to call Wake Forest home.

These medical professionals continue to be members of my team to this day, including my internist (who was suggested by a neighbor rather than my sister, who hadn't seen a general practitioner in years), neurologist, orthopaedist, and cardiologist. But I've also added an orthopaedic knee surgeon who played for the Minnesota Vikings and has hands as large as an Easter ham, an orthopaedic foot and ankle surgeon who has normal-sized hands and a great psychologist. I'd like to point out that half of these folks are women—the ham-handed football player being an exception.

It was my neurologist who gave me a script to get a North Carolina handicap parking permit. My original tag was good for six years. When 2012 rolled around, I asked her for another script, to which she replied, "Why don't you just get a permanent handicap license plate?" I gave her my irrational explanation, which was, "If I get a permanent plate versus a six-year hang tag (rearview mirror permit), aren't I sort of giving up, saying there's no way on earth I'll be fully restored to pre-stroke physicality one day?" She sort of looked at me like I was delusional, and, in truth, what I said *was* delusional as there is no way I'll return to my old 2005 self. But somewhere in the back of my mind, I don't want to consider myself permanently disabled.

In 2015, Cristie had foot surgery and had to wear what is referred to as a medical shoe on her right foot to protect her from hitting her toe, which was a temporary home to a screw. Her surgeon started to give her the form to get a handicap parking permit (or, as I call it, Andicap parking) prior to the operation when I piped up and said she could use one of mine (I have two). The surgeon said, "Of course. What was I thinking?" In a weird way, this sort of hurt my feelings. It was as if she was saying, "Of course you don't need a handicap permit. Your crippled husband probably already has one." I completely know that's not what she was saying, but reread the last sentence in the previous paragraph.

Mind you, all of this was coming from someone who, at age five, accidentally tore a picture I'd colored on a piece of construction paper. My mother kindly taped it back together for me. A week later, I took the tape off, certain that tape worked like Band-Aids and the construction paper would be "healed," back in one piece.

While I am aware of the severity of my stroke, I often have this odd thought: "If I lived to tell about it, just how horrible could it have been?" Is that a different take on "That which doesn't kill you, only makes you stronger"? Either way, surviving a near-death experience has dramatically lessened my fear of death.

A couple of years ago, I had a conversation with a physical therapist in which we discussed the fact that people are capable of faking a limp. Hell, Dennis Weaver did exactly that for nine years playing Chester on *Gunsmoke*. But this got me thinking, *If a person is capable of faking a limp, can someone with a limp fake walking without one?* I've tried it on numerous occasions, and the answer is no, not really. What happens when I try walking without a limp is that other parts of my body have to compensate for what my left leg lacks, meaning I sort of bend awkwardly at the waist and my arms flail. So if I try to fake not having a limp, it looks like I have something else wrong with me.

Recently, I received a postcard from Acorda Therapeutics asking if I'd be interested in participating in a clinical trial "looking at the safety and effectiveness of an investigational medication for the treatment of walking difficulties in people who have had an ischemic stroke at least six months ago." It turns out my neurologist gave my name to the research department at her practice who, in turn, passed my name on to Acorda Therapeutics, the company running what is known as the Milestone Study/Trial. My doctor, while more than qualified to treat stroke patients, specializes in treating multiple sclerosis patients, and the drug being tested, Ampyra, is used today by people with MS and Parkinson's disease to aid in walking. I called the number on the postcard and stated I'd be willing to participate, and was told someone would be contacting me in the near future. My walking gait is affected by more than just the stroke. You have to take into account my artificial left hip, a wired-together left patella and a right ankle harboring a small handful of screws. Add it all together, and it's sort of amazing that I can walk at all. So I'm eager to start the clinical trial in a couple of months.

I already take a drug called baclofen that is primarily prescribed to improve muscle movement for people with MS or spinal cord conditions. It's the smallest tablet in the arsenal of pills I take, and on those rare occasions when I've missed a dose, I think, *How big of a deal could it be to have missed taking one tiny little pill?* But in truth, if I miss a dose, the spasticity in my left arm gets so severe that my left hand becomes contorted and goes into extremely painful cramps. The one odd side effect of baclofen is a buildup of mucus in my throat. I was first put on this drug when I was in the hospital and complained about having to constantly (exaggeration) clear my throat, which led to a visit from an ear, nose, and throat specialist late one night. I went off this drug for a few years, but my neurologist put me back on it when my left arm started to get very hypertonic (excessive tension of muscles), and she's increased the dosage a couple of times since. And yes, it does still cause me to have to frequently clear my throat, but that small disadvantage is far outweighed by the hypertonicity.

I have a T-shirt that features a cartoonish illustration of a tablet of paper with the heading "Things to Do before I Die," and below the heading it reads "1. Don't die." That's the whole graphic. I think about that often. If I live long enough, how many phone calls about potential clinical trials might I receive? And how many of those trials or how many new therapies might actually lead to improvements in my quality of life?

Here I am nearly ten years down the road from that fateful sandwich. And now I do allow people to hold doors for me and am mindful to genuinely thank them for doing so. I do get pissed, however, when I hold doors for people and they *don't* say thank you—not because I have a disability but because it's rude. Periodically, strangers mistake the nature of my disability and thank me for my service to our nation in Vietnam. Usually, these people are actual veterans, and when I explain that I'm a stroke survivor with no military history at all, a moment of awkwardness ensues. I believe walking with a cane causes people to assume I'm older than I am. I have frequently received senior discounts I wasn't qualified to receive. Have I corrected these salespeople? Yeah, a few times.

I have a doctor (I won't say which discipline) whom I saw following the Femur Fiasco of '14, not because this doctor was following up on my femur surgery but because it was time for my annual appointment. While I like this physician, I feel my appointments last longer than necessary and the doctor tries very hard to be funny with me yet frequently fails. For example, when I saw him following the femur debacle, I asked hypothetically, "I had a stroke in my forties and hip replacement in my fifties. What are my sixties and seventies going to be like?" Without missing a beat, this doctor jokingly said, "Probably cancer then dementia." This he followed with a hearty laugh. And this was funny because …?

So here I am on a cruise and yesterday went on a shore excursion. Across the aisle from me on the bus traveling to a Canadian lighthouse was a gentleman with a walker wearing an "I'm a Vietnam Vet" baseball cap who had a very nasty cough. After walking around said lighthouse, I was climbing back on the bus when this gentleman extended his hand to help pull me up onto the bus. I told him, "No, thanks," not because I thought his disability trumped mine but because I was afraid of contracting whatever was causing his nasty cough.

It seems that most of my fellow passengers on this particular cruise are of the geriatric set and what interaction I've had with a few of these folks have involved many of them going on and on discussing their illnesses, ailments and recent surgeries. Seriously, if I ever become one of those people, please just …

Uh-oh, wait a minute.

Acknowledgments

My fourth-grade teacher, Mrs. Paula Garrett, was the first person to encourage me to write. A seventh-grade English teacher also encouraged my love of language, which eventually evolved from prose to journalism as I served as an editor for my high school newspaper.

Off to college in hopes of one day working in broadcast news (the actual profession, not the William Hurt, Albert Brooks, Holly Hunter movie), but I quickly learned I didn't have the stomach for the job after meeting a young reporter who had to interview the grandparents of a child who had died in an airplane crash. Fortunately, the advertising / public relations department was in the same building as the journalism school. And I thank the professors there at the University of South Carolina ("the *other* Carolina" now that I live in the Tar Heel State) for all they taught me.

Upon landing a job in advertising, I quickly gained several good mentors, among them Bill Westbrook, John Siddall and, of course, the late Mike Hughes. I wish to thank all the art directors I worked with whose tasteful design actually made people want to read my words. I especially salute Jerry Torchia, Shari Hindman, Carolyn McGeorge, Cabell Harris, Hal Tench, Diane Cook, Gregg Simonton, Bill Santry, Jim Mochnsky and the late Danny Boone. I also need to applaud the talented producers I've been fortunate enough to work with, including Craig Bowlus, Morty Baran, Sheila Fox, John Saag, Janet Mockard, Sandy Mislang, Judy Wittenberg, Merrick Murdock and Dana Cole. And then there are the writers I have worked with or have known who made me look over my shoulder more than once and inspired me to work harder. Thank you, Luke Sullivan, John

Mahoney, Jeanette Tyson, Sande Riesett, Patrick Scullin, Ken Marcus, Leslie Sims Cameron, Brian Kelley, Jeff McElhaney and David Oakley.

I wish to acknowledge those clients who trusted that I still had some talent in the ad world following my stroke. A special thank-you goes to Susan McFadden and Brenda Eddy.

I need to offer my deepest and most sincere thanks to the doctors, nurses, tech professionals, and wonderful therapists at Henrico Doctors' Hospital in Richmond, Virginia. Special tips of the hat to neurologist Cletus C. Aralu, MD; physical therapist Diana Wallace; and occupational therapist Stephanie Acree.

After Henrico Doctors', I encountered great physical and occupational therapists at Health South on Fitzhugh Avenue in Richmond, where I went for outpatient services. I remember one therapist in particular named Penny who was the most physically fit person I've ever met in my life. Plus she was a great, encouraging PT. Other good therapists were there as well; however, I don't remember everyone's name. It was at Health South that I had aquatic therapy for the first time, which I found very helpful in regaining the muscles required to walk as water offers resistance to help build muscle while taking away the danger of falling.

Upon moving to North Carolina, I continued outpatient rehab at WakeMed's Raleigh Campus. Again, I am ashamed I can't remember everyone's name, but I was blessed by great physical therapists, their aides, and two wonderful occupational therapists, including Tom Murdy, another extremely fit individual who had once worked as a bouncer at a mob-owned strip club in New Jersey. How this led him to the world of rehabilitation is anyone's guess.

From there, I was graduated to continue PT at a YMCA much closer to our house. There I met Wendy Phillips and her aide Ronnie Neal. Wendy, who is petite but amazingly strong, worked me harder than any previous therapist, and the results were obvious. Ronnie now works as a personal trainer at the Rex Wellness Center near our house. I returned to the Wendy & Ronnie Show after busting my patella. Despite all the work they put me through, we remain close friends to this day. Given that I frequently brought them fun-size Almond Joys when I came to therapy, I may have bought their friendship.

Following my knee surgery, the hospital sent a PT and an OT for in-home therapies. I was unimpressed with the physical therapist but was quite fond of the occupational therapist, Jim Woods. Little did I know that Jim and I would cross paths again seven years later following the Femur Fiasco of '14, when Jim returned to the house for another round of OT. Cristie and I have since become friends with Jim and his lovely wife, Annette. Jim's PT counterpart, Jeanne Guilliams, also came to the house a few days a week for therapy. It was probably about week three when Jeanne came in the back door and found me in the wheelchair at the kitchen table. I was feeling frustrated and generally pissed off about the whole situation. Jeanne immediately sensed this and said, "I was wondering how long you could go without this situation getting to you." She went on to say it was okay to get down every now and then and that she'd be wallowing in self-pity if she were in my shoes (or wheelchair). This snapped me out of my funk, and we went on with our routine. I will never forget her kindness.

In 2009 I wanted to return to occupational therapy just to see if there were any skills I could hone, and worked with Latonya Jamison at WakeMed. Besides working to improve the dexterity in my left hand, we traded several recipes. Every now and then she brought her daughter to work with her, and she is as good a mom as she is a therapist.

I previously mentioned my aquatic therapist, Rosemary Herlong, but want to blow another kiss of thanks in her direction.

It was a couple of years ago when my neurologist suggested I return to outpatient physical therapy just to see if there was anything that could be improved. That's when I met Connie Nehls, who, like Wendy, is small but strong and is also a very hands-on therapist. I went back to Connie for outpatient PT after I was able to bear weight on my left leg again following the femur break. I returned again last year when my left leg was still giving me problems. She's a great therapist and a lovely person.

And even after writing a chapter titled "MD Doesn't Stand for Medical Deity," there are several doctors, in addition to Dr. Aralu, who I would like to sincerely thank. Especially orthopaedic foot and ankle surgeon Sarah E. DeWitt, MD; orthopaedic surgeon Lyman S. W. Smith, MD; neurologist Susan A. Glenn, MD, PhD; psychologist Cynthia L. Frazier, PhD; dentist Robbie T. Smith, DDS; dental hygienist Robin Zeigler; and my internist Susheel V. Atree, MD.

I also need to thank everyone who encouraged me to write this book, including many of the medical professionals and therapists I've already acknowledged. Thank you, Suzanne Lucey, for introducing me to Alice Osborn, and thank you, Alice, for getting me to buckle down and finish this puppy. From my church, I'd like to thank Pastor James T. Roberson III, Pastor Peter Rochelle, Hal and JoAnne Drane (who were on their way to our house with lunch when my femur broke and turned around and went to the hospital to be there for Cristie), Clyde Alston (who came to the house three times while I was recovering from the femur debacle to trim my beard and did so with unmatched precision), and the rest of our Church on the Rock family who brought meals, came to visit, and offered up prayers. In addition, I'd like the folks at Cobble Hill Bed and Biscuit, especially Kylene Whitley, who is no longer there, for being so accommodating about boarding our dog when Cristie was away from home tending to me, and Lezlie, Misty, Mark and Chef Tom at Main Street Grille for the cookies and quiche.

I'd like to thank my cousins, both Massey and Ellis, as well as my stepsons and their families. I'm sad that my parents and my sister aren't here to share this book. My mother and father were always very encouraging in whatever endeavor I undertook. And my sister, Charlotte, played cheerleader to anything I wrote. I love and miss them very much.

I'm certain I've forgotten someone important, and if it's *you*, I am truly sorry. My excuse? I had a brain injury.

Finally, I thank you for actually reading this. If you are recovering from a serious medical event or love or care for such a person, I lift a glass to you. With my right hand.